GW00597234

1916 DREAM&DEATH

EDITORIAL

MANAGING EDITOR
Nick Maxwell

COMMISSIONING AND CONSULTING
EDITOR
Tommy Graham

EXECUTIVE AND PICTURE EDITOR
Joseph Culley

EDITORIAL BOARD
Tony Canavan
Elma Collins
Peter Collins
Patrick Fitzgerald
Brian Hanley
Angus Mitchell
Éamonn Ó Ciardha
Eamon O'Flaherty
Thomas O'Loughlin

PUBLISHING MANAGER
Nick Maxwell

DESIGN
Ger Garland

CARTOGRAPHY
Tomás Ó Brogáin

COPY-EDITING
Emer Condit

SALES/ PROMOTION/
MARKETING/ PRINT

ADMINISTRATION & SUBSCRIPTIONS
helen@wordwellbooks.com

ADVERTISING
una@wordwellbooks.com

PRINTED IN IRELAND BY
Turners, Longford

A *History Ireland* annual
FIRST PUBLISHED BY HISTORY
PUBLICATIONS LTD 2016,
Unit 9, 78 Furze Road, Sandyford
Industrial Estate, Dublin 18.
T. (+ 353 1) 2933568
F. (+ 353 1) 2939377
W. www.historyireland.com

ISBN 978-0-9935328-0-1

Preface

It was recently estimated—how accurately v
about 500 titles in print on the subject of 1916 and the
would *History Ireland* want to add to that number, particularly when we have
published so many articles (and even a previous special issue) devoted to
this topic?

Although we see a lot of good titles in the trade at the moment there isn't much out there that is suitable for the general reading public. *History Ireland* has always tried to give a sense of the past while offering a contemporary edge and has aimed at a wide range of readers, from professionals to those with a passing interest in history. It tries to be an essential read for all, with a high standard of writing and inclusion of up-to-the-minute research by leading historians. So it occurred to us that we should try to bring these qualities to bear on the subject of the 1916 Easter Rising.

We were also keen to consider the wider effects of the Rising, its aftermath, its literary legacy and its historiography. It likewise seemed logical that women (both combatant and non-combatant) and civilians (including children) deserved more of a voice than has perhaps been heard heretofore in publications aimed at the general public. The people who made up the Crown forces (army and police)—some of their stories as poignant as those on the side of the Republic—should be included in this kind of view.

Finally, we thought that two of the major figures most associated with the Rising should be considered in the light of today's scholarship and also though the lens of 50 years ago.

The result you have in front of you. We assembled a cast of experts to throw new light on this much-picked-over subject. To name but a few, we have Joost Augusteijn and Emmet O'Connor re-examining Pearse and Connolly respectively; Joseph Connell and John Gibney look at the events themselves; Mary McAuliffe and Lucy McDiarmid champion the women involved; and Joe Duffy, in a version of an earlier *History Ireland* article, remembers the children killed and wounded during the fighting.

In this special issue we have set about commemorating, memorialising, remembering, analysing and, to some extent, setting the record straight. We should not as a nation be afraid of recalling, with pride, awe, sadness and, yes, even some regret, the events that have shaped our present. If nothing else, recalling the events of 1916 could lay a useful platform from which the country can examine its achievements and failures over the last 100 years. We live in hope.

***

We at *History Ireland* would like to express our grateful thanks to all those whose personal efforts helped make this publication possible—in particular Conor McNamara (NUI Galway), Lorcan Collins, Bernie Metcalf and other members of staff at the National Library of Ireland, Richard Weinacht (Photographic Department, National Museum of Ireland), Jeff Wilson and Ruth Hegarty (Royal Irish Academy), Aoife Torpey (Kilmainham Gaol), Brian Kirby (Irish Capuchin Provincial Archives) and all the contributors, who provided copy in a timely and, indeed, enthusiastic fashion. It should be noted that every effort has been made to obtain permission for images that may be subject to copyright; if we have omitted to obtain any permissions, please contact us and we will rectify the situation in later editions.

Joe Culley, Tommy Graham, Nick Maxwell

1916 DREAM&DEATH

POSTSCRIPT

COVER: Irish Citizen Army volunteers on the roof of Liberty Hall. (Lorcan Collins)

BACK COVER: British soldiers in Henry Street after the Rising. (National Library of Ireland)

41

During this encounter Constable Patrick Whelan was shot dead. It believed that Whelan knew his attackers and was endeavouring talk to them when he was shot.

'Seven children were killed in the area arour the fruit market alone, making the Church Str environs the bloodiest spot for children durin Easter Week'

62

19

IT WAS NOT ONLY
PEARSE'S IDEAS ON
PATRIOTISM,
SACRIFICE, WAR AND
REDEMPTION THAT
FITTED IN WITH
EUROPEAN CURRENTS.
HIS THINKING IN ALL
AREAS WAS OFTEN
DIRECTLY INSPIRED
BY EUROPEAN
COUNTERPARTS.

25

8

HISTORY IRELAND

www.historyireland.com

WHAT'S THE STORY?

BY **THEO DORGAN**

There is always and everywhere, in each of us, a deep-rooted human need for some final version of our life story, and over against this a terrible sense of being overwhelmed by the sheer weight and variousness of that past we only dimly glimpse in all its roiling confusions.

Made anxious by the knowledge of our own mortal natures, we are always trying to settle our accounts, to get things straight before we are swept away—and what is true of the individual is also true, if perhaps in a more complex way, of the society in which, as individuals, we are inescapably implicated.

We are story-telling creatures, and stories are all we have to shore us up against our ruin. We are narrative-makers by nature and nurture; that is to say, we are editors of the actual as it appears to us—which is rarely, if ever, how it appears to others. We are always biased, no matter how much we protest other-

wise. No two people involved in a drama will tell the same story of what happened; we know this in our daily lives and yet we persist in our quaint belief that an adequate, all-encompassing account of the past is somehow possible. This is the marsh light, the will-o'-the-wisp that dances out ahead of all drawn to write history, tempting even the most sober of individuals to hope that they can present us with some full truth of what actually happened. The most naïve version of this impulse, and in some ways the most touching, is the stubborn belief that we can somehow own and complete the past by excavating and holding up to the light the evidence of fact.

The origin of history, as discipline and as practice, is rooted in a profound desire to know how we came to our present predicament. The self-set task of the historian is to determine the actuality of the past, to set it down in a coherent narrative so that we may, if we wish, draw certain conclusions about how the present moment came to be what it is. I hope it does not need saying that the historian, formed by her or his own personal history, can never hope to attain the objectivity of the physicist or chemist—even allowing that the truths of chemistry and physics are themselves susceptible to radical change. The historian is a particular kind of storyteller, disciplined, of course, by the imperatives of such facts as can be ascertained; but as a storyteller, inescapably, the historian is also an editor, an interpreter, an author of versions.

Bias is an ugly word when it carries a particular imputation, the freight of suggestion that a biased writer is somehow acting in bad faith, but the word as it derives from the Greek *epikarsios* means no more than 'oblique'; it can also mean 'pre-

●

disposition' or 'directing influence'. In these latter senses, to say that a history exhibits bias carries, to my mind, little or no negative connotation—as long as the author of a particular history makes no pretension to definitive objectivity beyond a claim of accuracy as regards matters of fact.

The stories that follow are just that, stories, each of them carrying a useful burden of fact, told on the bias, each of them a spur to thought and reflection, perhaps even to a revision of what the reader may have previously thought or believed; but equally they are just stories, more accurately *versions* from the past, because each is, in its own way, a retelling of narratives grand and small that have been carried forward through time by their keepers. The keepers may have been archivists, poets, grannies remembering a scrap of family lore, protagonists committing memory to paper—or, indeed, professional historians. What matters is the continuing or new life in the story, both in the gathering of facts and in their interpretation.

All history is a negation of time's onward imperative, a refusal to be governed by the demands of the living moment in all its overwhelming actuality, a refusal to bow down to the tyranny of the single, linear, forward-driving narrative. We are not bound by the past, any more than we are free to deny it. What matters is how we understand the past, and the presence of the past in the living moment. The more we read, the more we listen, the more we contribute as storytellers ourselves, the more we will understand of our human predicament. Inevitably, this means that we must learn to live with competing narratives, contradictions, evolutions of understanding, the permanent presence of changing perspectives.

All good stories amplify time, and our sense of ourselves as more densely present in time than day-to-day experience grants us. None of this is to say that we are free to invent the past; we are not free to say that something did not happen if we all know that it did. Neither is

it permissible to indulge in the counterfactual except as explicitly acknowledged speculation. When Yeats, somewhat forlornly, expressed the hope that England might yet keep faith, we who know that England did not in fact keep faith cannot presume to say that had this or that been the case they inevitably would have. That is to step outside the bounds of the story, to recruit the past to the service of a desired fiction—inevitably to excuse or promote an ideological position.

The business of history is to illuminate our understanding of the past, in all good faith. The process is essentially worthless if that understanding does not also illuminate the present from which we must shape our futures.

The only imaginable master narrative is a fluid, constantly changing, morphing and mutating narrative, one that contains and is comfortable with contradictions, a story inside which new stories are constantly arriving, old stories are constantly being retold, and changing in the telling. It is necessary to bring forward accurate records of the past, of life as it actually happened; it is equally necessary to frame, interrogate and meditate on these facts inside new narrative structures, to allow always for radical departures in understanding, to make stories that reflect and sometimes reconcile contradictions, real and apparent. The articles that follow are stories of that kind and, as such, should be read as extensions in the living moment of the master narrative we hunger for but can never, quite, trust. Tomorrow we move on, as that peculiar republican John Milton has it, 'to fresh woods and pastures new'.

Theo Dorgan
Dublin, January 2016

Theo Dorgan is a poet, writer, translator, librettist and editor. He is a member of Aosdána and served on the Boards of Triskel Arts Centre, Irish Writers Centre, Project Arts Centre, Ireland Literature Exchange and the African Cultural Project, among others.

SETTING THE SCENE

FAILURE TO PLAN

BY **JOHN GIBNEY**

CASEMENT SUBMITTED DETAILED PROPOSALS FOR AN EXPEDITIONARY FORCE TO THE GERMANS.

Image: John Lavery's *High Treason 1916* (oil on canvas, some 7ft x 10ft). The painting was commissioned from the Belfast artist by Judge Darling, who is seen presiding during Roger Casement's August appeal against his conviction for high treason. During the appeal Casement wrote to his family, asking 'Who was the painter in the jury box?' (© UK Government Art Collection)

What did Tom Clarke and his fellow conspirators actually have in mind?

WHAT MIGHT HAVE BEEN

Was there a plan for the Easter Rising, and what might have happened had it succeeded? These questions lurk on the fringes of much commentary on the events that actually took place. We know that a relatively small number of insurgents seized a selection of buildings in Dublin and proclaimed an independent Irish republic, and Dublin can be said to have gone to war over the next six days, with devastating consequences. Skirmishes took place in Meath and east Galway, Enniscorthy was briefly seized and large numbers of prospective insurgents assembled in Cork. But that was the extent of the Easter Rising; it was most certainly not a countrywide rebellion.

Nor was it the rebellion that seems to have been planned: the abortive attempt to import weapons from Germany on the *Aud*, Eoin MacNeill's attempt to countermand the mobilisation of the Irish Volunteers and the change of date from Easter Sunday to Easter Monday all point (as Joe Lee has argued) towards a very different Easter Rising from the rebellion that did take place.

●
Right: Roger Casement with veteran Fenian John Devoy in America in 1914. Devoy was leader of Clan na Gael, the main Irish-American nationalist organisation. In 1903 he had established the *Gaelic American* newspaper, of which Tom Clarke was assistant editor for a time. Earlier in 1914, Devoy had promoted a lecture tour of the US by Patrick Pearse to save St Enda's school. He then funded Casement's mission to Germany to procure arms and to recruit Irish prisoners of war. He was fully aware of plans for a revolt, as he was close to Clarke, Pearse and Joseph Plunkett.
(Image: Joseph McGarrity Collection. Digital Library@Villanova University)

Yet these certainties about the events and outcomes should be contrasted with the persistent uncertainty about what the insurrection was supposed to achieve and what its architects had planned. A great deal of attention over the years has been devoted to the alleged spiritual ambitions of the Rising as a form of 'blood sacrifice' aimed at resurrecting Irish nationhood, but surely its elevation into a metaphysical struggle in which military defeat was irrelevant is a neat way of rationalising that defeat? The swift execution of its leaders and the silencing of any plans they may have made only encouraged such thinking.

So, what did Thomas Clarke and his fellow conspirators actually have in mind? The clandestine planning and the swift execution of those who did the planning means that we can never know for certain. We can, however, seek clues from such scattered fragments of testimonies as have survived. This runs the risk of engaging in counterfactual speculation, which is no substitute for evidence; nevertheless, in the absence of enough evidence, it is better than nothing. And if we are going to speculate about what was supposed to have happened, we might as well begin with a concrete source: the lengthy memorandum that Roger Casement and Joseph Mary Plunkett submitted to the German authorities in early 1915, often referred to as the 'Ireland Report'. This set forth detailed proposals for how weapons for as many as 40,000 prospective Volunteers and an expeditionary force could land at the Shannon estuary and establish a base there. The weapons could then be distributed along the coast to facilitate insurrections along the western seaboard that would complement the rebellion in Dublin.

Casement and Plunkett were greatly exaggerating the potential for an uprising to a sceptical German audience (their claims stood in stark contrast to the view of the

Irish Rebellion_ May 1916.
A group of Officers with the captured rebel flag.

National Museum of Ireland

martyrdom, but a willingness to die for Ireland could coexist with a desire to stage a successful insurrection; these ambitions were not mutually exclusive.

After the Rising, some participants tried to make sense of what they had been involved in. According to Dublin Volunteer and academic Liam Ó Bríain, who attempted to piece together various fragments recorded from fellow veterans, the Rising was originally to focus on two key areas: Dublin for political purposes, as a rallying-cry of sorts, and Kerry for military purposes, with weapons being ferried north from there. Many Volunteers recalled that the west was to be a stronghold. It is worth noting that figures such as Ó Bríain and others all felt (in hindsight) that, at some level, martyrdom and a preparedness to sacrifice themselves played a part in the considerations of those who had planned the rebellion— regardless of whether such sentiments were representative of the rank and file. But the *sense* of a general military plan, however vague, was perhaps essential to stiffening the resolve of the rank and file by tapping into their aspirations to be soldiers, a plan to get something started—a means, as Ó Bríain put it, to 'a blood sacrifice made in Ireland'. Ó Bríain concluded, however, that 'probably the leaders had no further plans; that subsequent movements would be dictated by circumstances'.

Localised plans did exist outside of Dublin, but senior Volunteers such as Florence O'Donoghue of Cork felt that there was no coordinated strategy and that such a plan as did exist was related to gunrunning (in the form of the *Aud*'s cargo) rather than to a rebellion. Similar plans for obtaining and transporting weapons could be found in Limerick and Kerry. According to the Wexford Volunteer leader W.J. Brennan-Whitmore (who was, like Ó Bríain, sceptical of the notion that there was a well-defined national strategy), there were plans to disrupt communications and rail lines in the south-east: towns such

authorities, who perceived a country at peace rather than on the brink of open revolt). Their lengthy memorandum ultimately failed to convince. Its existence is not in itself proof that there was a coherent, overall plan for the Easter Rising (nor even that it was a good plan), but some key provisions of the 'Ireland Report' echo what hap-

●

Top: A group of British army officers posing with the flag of the Irish Republic (above) at the Parnell Monument after the surrender. (Image courtesy of UCD Digital Library from an original in UCD Special Collections)

pened, or was supposed to happen, in April 1916. The attempt to land weapons, and the plans to distribute them in the west, correspond with what some Irish Volunteers later claimed was to have taken place had the Germans got on board. (That said, some of these contemporaries had strong reservations about the alleged plans.) The 'Ireland Report' does give an insight into how some of those who planned the Rising thought they might stage it—and win. Some of the 1916 leaders may well have been prepared to welcome

Dublin Volunteer and academic Liam Ó Bríain, who attempted to piece together various fragments recorded from fellow veterans, said that the Rising was originally to focus on two key areas: Dublin for political purposes, as a rallying-cry of sorts, and Kerry for military purposes, with weapons being ferried north from there.

as New Ross and Rosslare were obvious venues for British landings should reinforcements be dispatched to Ireland (in the end British troops landed in Dublin with ease). Transport links between Dublin, the Curragh (which contained the largest military base in Ireland) and the Protestant north-east were also to be cut; it was vaguely felt that these measures would deprive the British military in Dublin of reinforcements, and would buy time for the distribution of weapons from the *Aud*.

All of this is a moot point, for the weapons never landed and this phantom rising never came to pass.

That said, speculation about alternative outcomes might shed some light on concrete realities. So let us make a crucial assumption: the cargo of the *Aud* is landed and distributed. The Volunteers could then attempt to establish an armed presence along the west coast from Cork to Sligo, with the River Shannon acting as a natural barrier, and they might even reach into the midlands. Admittedly, all that was coming from Germany were 20,000 Russian rifles, ten machine-guns and 5,000,000 rounds of ammunition that could not easily be replenished, which poses serious questions regarding how long they could have held out. There may not have been a German expeditionary force but the guns were still to be delivered and could yet be distributed in the

manner suggested above.

The British garrison in Ireland had been eroded by the requirements of the war, though it would have been reinforced rapidly had a larger rebellion broken out. This is what happened in Dublin, though it took a number of days.

So let us engage in some more conjecture. The insurgent plans in Dublin were, up to a point, sound *in theory*, owing to the location of defensive positions that could block major routes and infrastructure, but not in practice, owing to their numerical weakness and scarcity of weapons. In other words, in this scenario, in which insurgents along the west coast stage an action with an ill-defined set of objectives (along the lines of what did happen in east Galway), this speculative rising in Dublin would be no different to what did happen (a possibility implied in the 'Ireland Report'). The distinction lies in what might have happened elsewhere: what if the guns *had* landed? Had these weapons been distributed across the west and south, and into the midlands, *then* what would have happened? And how long could the Volunteers have sustained themselves if they had risen outside Dublin?

The British mobilised large numbers of troops rapidly to crush the real rebellion, and there is no reason to believe that this could not have been continued. And in the circumstances it was inevitable that the British would seek to crush the revolt lest the Germans think twice of having washed their hands of it, which they had in effect done by April 1916.

This, however, excludes the possibility that a prolonged rebellion, along the lines suggested by Ó Bríain, might have reignited German interest before the battle of Jutland. Or would the *perception* of a widespread rising have prompted the sort of excessive reaction from the British forces as was seen in Dublin, regardless of the reality on the ground? In time of war, it is inconceivable that Britain would not have responded on a disproportion-

ately greater and more ruthless scale (though perhaps with an eye on US opinion as they did so). But would their activities have alienated the locals? How would Home Rule supporters and Redmondites have stood in relation to what could be painted as an invasion, if it were to happen on a sustained scale across large swathes of territory? The British army held Dublin, and the continued loyalty of Belfast would have ensured that both cities could still be used as entry points for troops. Indeed, how would Unionist Ulster have responded to such a turn of events? Even if sympathy and support were garnered by the Volunteers—and the experience of places such as Galway City ('the most Shoneen town in Ireland') suggests that such support was

● Above: Irish Volunteer Captain Robert Monteith went to Berlin with Casement to attempt to recruit soldiers for a 'Casement Brigade' from among Irish prisoners of war. The Irish soldiers proved reluctant, however, and the 'Casement Brigade' never numbered more than 60 men.

NO PARADES!

Irish Volunteer Marches Cancelled

A SUDDEN ORDER.

The Easter manoeuvres of the Irish Volunteers, which were announced to begin to-day, and which were to have been taken part in by all the branches of the organisation in city and country, were unexpectedly cancelled last night.

The following is the announcement communicated to the Press last evening by the Staff of the Volunteers:—

April 22, 1916.

Owing to the very critical position, all orders given to Irish Volunteers for to-morrow, Easter Sunday, are hereby rescinded, and no parades, marches, or other movements of Irish Volunteers will take place. Each individual Volunteer will obey this order strictly in every particular.

EOIN MACNEILL,
Chief of Staff,
Irish Volunteers.

vived, to attempt to tease out the nuances of what the leaders of the Rising had hoped to achieve and how they might have hoped to achieve it, however realistic or otherwise their goals were perceived to be at the time—and without the benefit of hindsight.

Further reading

J. Gibney, 'What if the guns had landed? Another version of Casement's Easter Rising', *Breac* 4 (on-line).

Above left: Eoin MacNeill, professor of early Irish history at University College Dublin, co-founder of the Gaelic League and chief of staff of the Irish Volunteers. As MacNeill was not a member of the IRB, he was unaware of their plans for a rebellion. When in Easter Week he learned of them, and of Casement's plan to land arms, he initially acquiesced. When he learned of Casement's arrest, however, he issued a countermanding order to the Volunteers to stop their mobilisation on Easter Sunday. (UCD Archives)

Above: MacNeill's countermanding order to stop the planned mobilisation of the Irish Volunteers on Easter Sunday, 23 April.

unlikely—their limited munitions would not have lasted for long. Even in this reading, it is hard not to expect the British to win this alternative Easter Rising.

But it could have taken them a while to do so, and what would the political cost have been? As Ó Bríain argued (with the benefit of hindsight), 'Had the volunteers of 1916 been able to produce for a few months in the summer of 1916 the state of affairs which existed here in 1920–21 ... A few months of guerilla warfare, and I for one could visualise correspondence, a truce, negotiations, a settlement, all taking place in 1916.' After all, his belief that

Ireland might get a hearing at a post-war peace conference was held by some of those who fought. The British Empire's difficulty might yet have been Ireland's opportunity.

This, of course, is fanciful, as all such speculation is bound to be, and the centenaries being marked are the centenaries of what actually happened rather than what might have been. Nevertheless, such speculation can at times help to shed light on obscure areas of the past. The complexities and nuances of the Easter Rising have been examined minutely in recent years. But it is also a useful exercise, within the limits of the evidence that has sur-

EASTER WEEK

BY **JOSEPH E.A. CONNELL JR**

Fire is the quickest and best way to get insurgents out of buildings, and it was the fires throughout the centre of Dublin that brought the Volunteers to ruin.

Image: Prince's Street ran between the Hotel Metropole (the rubble in the foreground) and the GPO. The artillery shelling and the resulting fires ruined them both and much of the surrounding area. On Easter Monday morning, Michael Collins came here to escort Joseph Plunkett to the GPO. (National Library of Ireland)

It began formally at noon on Easter Monday. By the time of the surrender on Saturday around 450 people had been killed.

A BRIEF HISTORY OF A REBELLION

The IRB Military Council, consisting of Thomas Clarke, Patrick Pearse, James Connolly, Seán MacDermott, Éamonn Ceannt, Thomas MacDonagh and Joseph Plunkett, scheduled the Rising for 6.00 p.m. on Easter Sunday, 23 April 1916. Pearse issued an order on 8 April for a general mobilisation on that day. This order was issued publicly and with the full authorisation of the Irish Volunteer executive in order to deceive the Dublin Castle authorities into believing that it was just a by-now-routine route march exercise.

On Holy Saturday the Military Council knew that their plans had been severely compromised by the loss of a ship from Germany, the *Aud*. It was loaded with weapons, but its arrival at Fenit, Co. Kerry, and delivery of arms was foiled owing to failures in communications.

US-based Fenian John Devoy had asked the Germans for 100,000 rifles, artillery pieces and German officers, but the Germans sent just 20,000 rifles, ten machine-guns and the necessary ammunition.

The *Aud* arrived off the Kerry coast as originally scheduled on Holy Thursday. Its captain, Lt Karl Spindler, had been instructed to look for two green lanterns as a signal from the shore. The Volunteers on shore, however, acting according to a revised schedule, had been told to look for the ship's signal on the evening between Holy Saturday and Easter Sunday. On Good Friday night, Spindler weighed anchor to flee the Irish coast, but the ship was soon overtaken by the Royal Navy. The British decided to escort the *Aud* to Queenstown (Cobh) Harbour, but Spindler knew that the ruse had failed and scuttled her.

When Eoin MacNeill, O/C of the Volunteers, found that he had been deceived about the Rising, including the 'Castle Document' (alleged plans by the authorities to pre-empt any move by the Irish Volunteers), the news of Roger Casement's capture in Tralee and the loss of the *Aud*, it led him to cancel the manoeuvres scheduled for Easter.

'Owing to the very critical position, all orders given to Irish Volunteers for tomorrow, Easter Sunday, are hereby rescinded, and no parades, marches, or other movements of Irish Volunteers will take place. Each individual Volunteer will obey this order strictly in every particular.'

But the Rising's leaders determined that to delay further would be fatal for their plans, and so the Rising was rescheduled. The Military Council made two equally important decisions: first, they sent dispatches immediately to the various commands, *confirming* MacNeill's cancellation of that day's manoeuvres; second, they decided that the Rising would commence the next day at noon.

So at noon on Easter Monday, 24 April 1916, approximately 800 Volunteers and 200 Irish Citizen Army (ICA) members stormed buildings in central Dublin and declared an independent Irish Republic. The Irish plan had two elements: first, to prevent British access to the city centre from the major military barracks or from Kingstown; second, to maintain a line of communication between Dublin and the country. They hoped to keep open a corridor out of Dublin. They chose their positions carefully, forcing the British to attack, as the rebels were holding the capital city of Ireland, and in the hope that they could hold out for long enough to attract international attention as a rebellion rather than just as a mere riot.

Joseph Plunkett was the primary planner of the military actions, along with James Connolly. Neither Plunkett nor Connolly was a trained

●

Below from left: The seven signatories of the Proclamation and members of the IRB Military Council: Patrick Pearse, Seán MacDermott, Thomas MacDonagh, Thomas Clarke, James Connolly, Éamonn Ceannt and Joseph Plunkett.

Eight other rebels were executed in May—Con Colbert, Edward Daly, Seán Heuston, John MacBride, Michael Mallin, Michael O'Halloran, William Pearse and Thomas Kent—while Roger Casement was hanged in London in August. (National Library of Ireland)

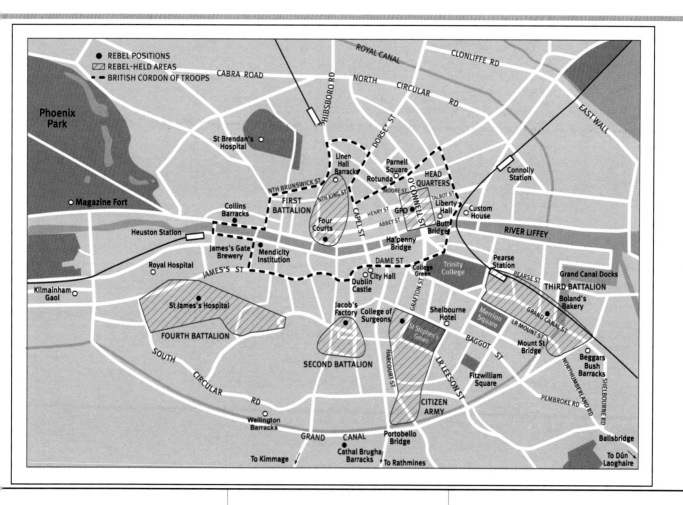

REBEL POSITIONS
REBEL-HELD AREAS
BRITISH CORDON OF TROOPS

military strategist, and since 1916 most have challenged whether the plan was militarily sound. In particular, it has been questioned whether the Volunteers and Citizen Army should have taken the buildings they did, whether a static defensive plan could have been successful, and whether their intent to engage in urban warfare could have achieved their aims.

While there was little hope of defeating the British army, the planners of the Rising felt that international opinion would soon force the British to come to terms with the rebels and to give independence to the country. Éamonn Ceannt told his wife, Áine: 'If we last a month they—the British—will come to terms'.

So the Irish strategy must be considered a failure. Nevertheless,

●
Above: The vast majority of the fighting during the week was confined to the area between Dublin's canals, in a radius from the GPO of less than three kilometres. (O'Brien Press)

although the overall strategy of the Volunteers was suspect, the urban tactics employed were quite advanced for their time.

In the end the British had to use artillery (and the fires which resulted) to remove most defenders from their entrenched positions; this destroyed much of the centre of Dublin and inflicted significant losses on civilians. It should be emphasised that the incendiary shells that the British used were more effective in ending the Rising than were high-explosive shells. Fire is the quickest and best way to get insurgents out of buildings, and it was the fires throughout the centre of Dublin that brought the Volunteers to ruin. While the Volunteers had considered the danger of fire, and while many means were taken to douse fires as they occurred, it was the flammability of the oils and chemicals in shops and stores around the centre of Dublin, as well as the flammability of the buildings themselves and their fixtures, which made their defensive positions so

vulnerable. Ultimately, the fires succeeded in forcing the evacuation of buildings and were the primary cause of the surrender.

After capturing the General Post Office (GPO) on Sackville Street, Pearse read the *Proclamation of the Provisional Government of the Irish Republic* in front of that landmark building.

The British military reacted quickly at the outset of firing. Their immediate objectives were to recapture the Magazine Fort in Phoenix Park, to secure the Viceregal Lodge in Phoenix Park, to relieve and strengthen the garrison in Dublin Castle, and to get reinforcements from Irish garrisons and from England. The first reinforcements from the 3rd Reserve Cavalry Brigade arrived at Kingsbridge Station at 4.15 p.m., and troops continued to arrive there and at Amiens Street Station on Tuesday. The British initiated actions to relieve Dublin Castle and made certain of the security of the barracks throughout Dublin, as

well as other positions on the perimeter of the rebellion. By Monday night a scheme for the transport of troops from Liverpool had been drawn up.

Then the British put their efforts into securing the approaches to their administrative headquarters at Dublin Castle and isolating the rebel headquarters in the GPO. By early Tuesday morning the British had taken the steps necessary to safeguard the Castle, secured the other barracks in Dublin, summoned additional reinforcements, and provided the basis for the offensive actions to follow which would lead to the defeat of the rebels.

Quickly the Crown forces greatly outnumbered the rebels, marshalling almost 20,000 troops by week's end in opposition to about 2,100 rebels. The British immediately

began their counterattacks, specifically directed toward the centre of the rebel positions in the GPO, and isolating each of the other garrisons at the same time. On Tuesday they began to control the area south of the Liffey, opening a corridor from Richmond Barracks to the Castle and then east to Trinity College.

After eliminating the threat to the Castle, the British attacked City Hall, and that garrison, along with its outlying positions, was taken by Tuesday evening. The Shelbourne Hotel was occupied in the pre-dawn hours of Tuesday, and when the hotel and the adjacent United Services Club were taken, the Citizen Army position in St Stephen's Green was untenable. Cmdt Michael Mallin's garrison withdrew to the College of Surgeons on the far side of the Green. Though they held that position

until the end, they were effectively isolated from the fighting. Also on Tuesday, the British established their headquarters in Trinity College and cut the rebel positions in two,

●

Above: British troops and Dublin policemen place barbed wire around City Hall to keep out the curious. The first casualty among 'combatants' was unarmed DMP Constable James O'Brien, shot dead at the neighbouring upper gate of the Castle Yard. His assailant, ICA Captain Seán Connolly, and his party retreated to the City Hall, where Connolly was soon shot dead while on the roof. (National Library of Ireland)

●

Opposite: British troops inspect a motor car on Mount Street Bridge, the scene of some of the bloodiest fighting. Two battalions of the Sherwood Foresters suffered 234 casualties, including 18 officers, as they tried to take the bridge, which connected Northumberland Road to Lower Mount Street across the Grand Canal. (National Library of Ireland)

REBELS

PATRICK PEARSE

BY **JOOST AUGUSTEIJN**

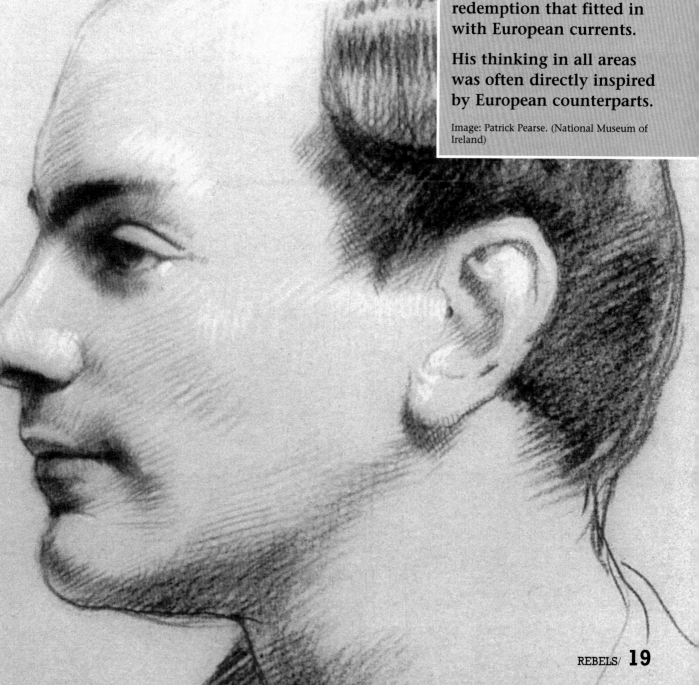

It was not only Pearse's ideas on patriotism, sacrifice, war and redemption that fitted in with European currents.

His thinking in all areas was often directly inspired by European counterparts.

Image: Patrick Pearse. (National Museum of Ireland)

Despite the popular perception, Pearse's thinking reflected and was heavily influenced by contemporary international thinking

THOROUGHLY MODERN MAN OF EUROPE

Whatever one's point of view, Patrick Pearse has always engendered strong emotions. Shortly after the Easter Rising he became widely revered, some even suggesting that he should be made a saint. In the decades surrounding the outbreak of the Troubles in Northern Ireland, however, he was frequently described as a 'fascist'. In 1978 Xavier Carty passionately condemned Pearse's celebration of the use of violence, and even argued that his writings 'indicate a narrow fanaticism as well as an obsession with racial purity and the pre-eminence of a mythical Gaelic race suggesting that if he had not died at Kilmainham he might have been an Irish Hitler'.

In recent years a more sophisticated view of Pearse has been developed in academic works, but in popular perception he is still seen as a proponent of doubtful ideas, while allusions to autism and homosexuality have also hit the headlines.

WHAT PEARSE SAID
The origins of this negative image of

Below: An example of Pearse's awareness of European developments is his use of the pageant as a means to impress mythological and heroic examples on his pupils. Here we see William Pearse (centre) with pupils performing 'Fionn, A Dramatic Spectacle'. (Pearse Museum, OPW)

PAGEANTS
The most visual part of Pearse's work in St Enda's was the staging of pageants. Ironically, pageants were originally used in religious ceremonies or to demonstrate the power of monarchs. For Pearse they had a clear function: 'we are anxious to send our boys home with the knightly image of Cúchulainn in their hearts and his knightly words ringing in their ears'. They also had a wider impact. When the whole cast of *The boy-deeds of Cúchulainn* marched through Dublin in costume in June 1909, a crowd gathered spontaneously and began to sing 'Who fears to speak of '98?'. This gave Thomas MacDonagh the feeling that the crowd 'expect us to lead them against the Castle'.

Pearse clearly lie in his writings. His sense of messianic duty associated with youth, rebirth and political violence indeed seems to come close to fascism. The most cited example for this stems from 1915, when he

welcomed the First World War:

'It is good for the world that such things should be done. The old heart of the earth needed to be warmed with the red wine of the battlefields. Such august homage was never before offered to God as this, the homage of millions of lives given gladly for love of country.'

It is not too difficult to find other examples of such extremism in his work, which, when put together, make for unsettling reading.

Much of this started with the strong emphasis on patriotism, which also permeated the curriculum presented to his pupils at St Enda's. In the school prospectus of 1908 their duties were clearly spelled out: 'It will be attempted to inculcate in the pupils the desire to spend their lives working hard and zealously for their fatherland and, if it should ever be necessary, to die for it'. Pearse felt that what he saw as a feminised society should recover the ideals of courage, strength and heroism. Through war, he argued, it was possible 'to restore manhood to a race that has been deprived of it'. In this the shedding of blood was even considered a good thing:

'I should like to see any and every body of Irish citizens armed. We must accustom ourselves to the thought of arms, to the sight of arms, to the use of arms. We may make mistakes in the beginning and shoot the wrong people; but bloodshed is a cleansing and a sanctifying thing.'

Only through war could Ireland be really freed from the English presence:

'It is evident that there can be no peace between the body politic and a foreign substance that has intruded itself into its system: between them war only until the foreign substance is expelled or assimilated'

Right: German socialist Karl Liebknecht. He said of the failed Spartakist uprising in 1919: '... they have shed blood for a holy cause, which has thus been sanctified'. (Library of Congress)

This was certainly a way of putting things which reminds one of Adolf Hitler and his attitude to Jews.

Pearse also compared the necessary sacrifices to that of Christ: 'It had taken the blood of the son of God to redeem the world. It would take the blood of the sons of Ireland to redeem Ireland.' And he compared the Irish people to the Messiah: '... the people labouring, scourged, crowned with thorns,

Below: Rabindranath Tagore, a Bengali polymath who reshaped Bengali literature and music.

TAGORE

Pearse had many international contacts, including Rabindranath Tagore, a Bengali nationalist and winner of the 1913 Nobel Prize for literature, who had also founded his own school, called Shantiniketan. After W.B. Yeats had called this school 'the Indian St Enda's', Pearse approached Yeats and it was decided to stage Pearse's play *An Rí* (The King) alongside Tagore's play *Dak-ghar* (The Post Office), directed by Yeats at the Abbey. Tagore subsequently asked Pearse to allow him to perform *An Rí* in his school. This was done, and Tagore later wrote to Pearse that he was delighted with the play.

agonising and dying, to rise again immortal and impassable'.

In his stories he took this a step further: 'One man can free a people as one man redeemed the world. I will go into battle with bare hands. I will stand up before the Gael as Christ hung naked before men on the tree.' To counter concerns that England could not be beaten militarily, he emphasised that God was on the Irish side in a reasoning that comes close to that of a jihadist.

'Always it is the many who fight for the evil thing, and the few who fight for the good thing; and always it is the few who win. For God fights with the small battalions. If sometimes it has seemed otherwise, it is because the few who have fought for the good cause have been guilty of some secret faltering, some infidelity to their best selves, some shrinking back in the face of a tremendous duty.'

To underline the extremism of this thinking, commentators have often pointed at James Connolly's reaction to Pearse's celebration of the 'red wine of the battlefields' in 1915:

ciated with dying as a soldier, and used the same metaphor as Pearse about a 'world grown old and cold and weary'. Among German officers at this time a cult of sacrifice developed in which they venerated fallen comrades who had shown 'boundless initiative, inordinate capacity for suffering and blind self-sacrifice'.

The celebration of patriotism had also become widespread in the education systems of many western countries in the late nineteenth century. The most notable example was the introduction of the Pledge of Allegiance in American schools in 1892. The praise of a short and heroic life was equally widely sung. Even James Joyce, who fled Ireland in part because of its narrow-minded nationalism, argued in his story *The dead* that it was better to 'pass boldly into that other world, in full glory of some passion, than fade and wither dismally with age'.

Winston Churchill espoused similar ideas in 1908: 'What is the use of living, if it be not to strive for noble causes and to make this muddled world a better place for those who will live in it after we are gone?'

The popularity of the operas of Wagner also attested to the celebration of the hero in mythology and the emphasis on manly virtues.

SOCIALISTS
Virtually every aspect of Pearse's thinking can be found among socialists of different hue at that time. In particular, since the Paris Commune of 1871 a militarisation of their thinking had taken place. Sacrifice, martyrdom, heroism and even redemption were emphasised. This can be seen most clearly in the statement made by Karl Liebknecht after the Spartakists' attempt at revo-

●

Above left: Patrick Pearse, on a platform, at a recruitment meeting for the Irish Volunteers, 1915. 'I will stand up before the Gael as Christ hung naked before men on the tree.' (National Library of Ireland)

●

Opposite: The funeral of Jeremiah O'Donovan Rossa on 1 August 1915 at Glasnevin Cemetery. (Glasnevin Trust)

'No, we do not think the old heart of the earth needs to be warmed with the red wine of millions of lives. We think anyone who does is a blithering idiot. We are sick of such teaching, and the world is sick of such teaching.'

Connolly, however, was certainly not representative of mainstream thinking in Europe at that time.

Indeed, if we look at contemporary public discourse we find surprising similarities with Pearse's ideas.

WIDESPREAD CULT OF SACRIFICE
During the First World War it was not uncommon to preach the heroism of war or the beauty of sacrifice. In his War Sonnets, the English poet Rupert Brooke emphasised the honour and nobility asso-

lution in Germany failed in 1919. He started off by saying that 'there were defeats which were victories; and victories which are more fatal than defeats', and then continued:

'They died gloriously; they fought for something higher, for the noblest goal of the suffering humanity, for the spiritual and material salvation of the starving masses, they have shed blood for a holy cause, which has thus been sanctified. And from every drop of their blood, this seed of dragons for the winners of today, will rise the fallen Avenger, from each damaged fibre new fighters for the higher cause, which is eternal and imperishable as the firmament. The vanquished of today will be the winners of tomorrow.'

If the starving masses are read as the Irish, this could easily have been said by Pearse directly after the Rising.

During the war the glorification of bloodshed as a cleansing experience was also widespread. Even a peace-loving man like Thomas Mann, who would later win the Noble Prize for literature and became an active opponent of the Nazis, described the war in 1914 as 'a purification, a liberation, an enormous hope'. In Ireland this also had a long pedigree. The popular Canon Sheehan wrote in 1914 in his novel *The graves at Kilmorna*: 'As the blood of martyrs was the seed of saints, so the blood of the patriot is the seed from which alone can spring fresh life into a nation that is drifting into the putrescence of decay'.

The comparisons to Christ and the road to redemption were also not uncommon. Even James Connolly, who was essentially an atheist, spoke about a rebellion in those terms: 'we recognise that of us, as of mankind before Calvary, it may truly be said "without the shedding of blood there is no redemption" '. The same applies to Liebknecht, who argued that 'still the road to Golgotha is not completed for the German workers—but the day of redemption is near'.

'MOVING AWAY FROM THE DUNGHEAP AND THE TURF-RICK'

It was not only Pearse's ideas on patriotism, sacrifice, war and redemption that fitted in with European currents. His thinking in all areas concurred with and was often directly inspired by European counterparts. Pearse read international newspapers and literature, and corresponded with a number of like-minded figures abroad. His emphasis on the language as a tool to regenerate Irish culture and nationality was based on foreign

dungheap and the turf-rick; let us throw off the barnyard muck'. In this attack on convention and false sentiments in literary writing Pearse was in tune with the contemporary literary sensibilities of Europe and America, which he knew well.

VIEWS ON EDUCATION

His international orientation also deeply influenced Pearse's thinking in the field of educational policy. He had come into contact with Welsh, Belgian and other international proponents of the New Education Movement, who all argued that the needs of individual children should be central in teaching and who opposed the restriction to the three 'R's. His actual policies were developed slowly by the study of educational theory and the practices in other countries. The special place that he gave to the inculcation of patriotism was, for instance, the result of his study of the educational system in the US. Much of his emphasis on the direct method and his use of modern teaching aids such as cut-out figures were directly inspired by his visit to Belgian schools in 1905.

A final example of Pearse's awareness of European developments is his use of the pageant as a means to impress mythological and heroic examples on his pupils. The popularity of public pageant and dramas based on historical themes was a pan-European phenomenon at that time. In one of the first editions of Pearse's school newspaper, *An Macaomh*, an article was reprinted dealing with the return of pageants to Europe. They subsequently became one of the main cultural activities in the school. In 1913 a public performance by the 'St Enda players' was clearly greatly anticipated by the Gaelic League newspaper: 'It may be assumed that the pageants & pageant plays will be the most beautiful things of the kind that have been in Dublin'.

The picture that emerges here clearly places Pearse in a European context. Most of his ideas were directly inspired or even borrowed from outside. His thinking was also

in no way conservative or retrograde. Apart from his extremist militarism and nationalism, which were widely shared, his ideas on educational and literary thinking were clearly modernist. They also concur with his radical ideas on workers' and women's rights. All this can lead to only one conclusion: that Pearse was an exponent of his time and represented ideas widely held in Europe and beyond.

Joost Augusteijn is a lecturer in European History at Leiden University. His Patrick Pearse: the making of a revolutionary *is published by Palgrave, Macmillan. This article first appeared in* History Ireland *Vol. 18, No. 6.*

Further reading

R. Higgins & R. Uí Chollatáin (eds), *The life and afterlife of P.H. Pearse. Pádraic Mac Piarais saol agus oidhreacht* (Dublin, 2009).

S. Ó Buachalla, *A significant Irish educationalist: the educational writings of P.H. Pearse* (Dublin, 1980).

● Above left: Willie Pearse. (National Library of Ireland)

● Above: In 1908 Winston Churchill wrote of the ideal of sacrifice: 'What is the use of living, if it be not to strive for noble causes and to make this muddled world a better place for those who will live in it after we are gone?'

examples and was shared with many separatist and regionalist movements throughout Europe: 'The moral of the whole story is that the Hungarian language revival of 1825 laid the foundation of the great, strong and progressive Hungarian nation of 1904. And so it shall fall out in Ireland.'

Although initially he argued that ancient Irish writers were even better than the writers from Greek and Roman antiquity, he soon became one of the strongest proponents of a modern literature in Irish. He believed that Irish literature should be taken from 'the Anglicised backwaters into the European mainstream'. He strongly criticised the focus on rural life by most Irish contemporary writers and called upon them to deal with the modern world: 'Let us move away from the

JAMES CONNOLLY

BY **EMMET O'CONNOR**

Lenin made the astute observation on Easter Week that the Irish *'rose prematurely, when the European revolt of the proletariat had not yet matured'*

Image: James Connolly (National Library of Ireland)

How did the Labour leader square his
radical socialism with nationalism?

RED AMONG THE GREEN

James Connolly was right in arguing that Labour should lead on the national question. If Labour wished to be a force in politics, it hardly made sense to ignore the big issue of the day, as it tried to do in 1918, or tag along behind others, as it did subsequently. One of the mysteries of Labour history is why, if Connolly made such common sense and was Labour's national martyr, a yawning posthumous gap opened between the *de jure* respect for his status and the *de facto* reluctance to apply his ideas. One explanation is that Labour was mentally colonised. Another possibility worth considering is that Connolly's thinking, too, was colonised.

Colonisation distorts by displacing the ordinary with the extraordinary choices of shooting or saluting the new masters. The first can lead to toxic obsession, the second to alienation from one's reality, as the colonised denigrate their own values as backward and attempt to fit themselves into the model of the metropolitan. To find a Labour mind-set not unbalanced by Anglophobia or Anglocentrism one needs to look beyond the Great Famine. When Daniel O'Connell raised the Repeal banner in 1830, trade unions promptly rallied round, convinced that Repeal was a prerequisite of democracy and economic recovery. Unions were not blind to O'Connell's anti-trade union views. Nor did they develop an abstruse theology about the true radical being a Repealer and vice versa. They took a simple, logical position that the Act of Union and free trade with Britain were the cause of the decline of Irish industry, that one couldn't protect wages in a declining economy, one couldn't end decline without tariffs, one wouldn't get tariffs without self-government, and 'the Liberator' was the only man who could deliver an Irish parliament.

The grim scenario feared by the unions came to pass. Post-Famine decades witnessed a paradox of economic decay and modernisation, which in the Ireland of the time meant Anglicisation. By the 1890s, when a withered trade unionism was considering the formation of a trades congress, Michael Davitt urged unions to form a primarily political federation and implement their agenda through an alliance with the Irish Parliamentary Party (IPP). Instead, they accepted the mainstream British view of Labour and nationalism as dichotomous and founded the Irish Trades Union Congress (ITUC). Modelled on its British namesake, the ITUC entailed a congress based on industrial organisation, where Labour was weak, rather than politics, where it had the potential to punch above its weight through the IPP. It also meant that the ITUC would keep the national question at arm's length and pursue a notional, strictly Labour politics; it was a self-denying ordinance that merely depoliticised the movement.

Born of impoverished Irish parents in Edinburgh in 1868 (he claimed to have been born in Monaghan), Connolly left school at the age of ten or eleven, slaved at menial jobs, joined and deserted the British army, and became secretary of the Scottish wing of the Social Democratic Federation (SDF), the leading British Marxist party. Through the SDF he secured a job as a political organiser for the Dublin Socialist Society. On arrival in Dublin in 1896, Connolly had his politics all worked out. With his cogency and energy, he turned the Dublin comrades into the Irish Socialist Republican Party (ISRP) and the tiny ISRP into a mighty mouse. After the pragmatic nationalism of trade unionists up to the 1890s, the growing perception of Labour and nationalism as dichotomous in the

Above: Head office of the ITGWU, Liberty Hall, adorned with banner stating 'James Connolly Murdered May 12th 1916'. (National Library of Ireland)

Opposite: James Connolly around 1890. Born of impoverished Irish parents in Edinburgh in 1868, Connolly left school at the age of ten or eleven, slaved at menial jobs, joined and deserted the British army, and became secretary of the Scottish wing of the Social Democratic Federation, the leading British Marxist party.

1880s and 1890s, the benign hope of moderate British groups like the Fabians and the Independent Labour Party—which enjoyed some support in Belfast—that the Irish problem would be resolved through social democracy, and the ultra-leftism of small Dublin socialist groups which dismissed nationalism as an epiphenomenon, the ISRP's socialist republicanism offered a fifth position on the national question. Despite its intended anti-colonialism, it stemmed from Connolly's background in the SDF rather than from Irish experience. There is a revealing parallel between his projection of Gaelic Ireland as a primitive communist society destroyed by Norman feudalism and Chartist efforts to represent the English as a 'free-born' people before their enslavement under the 'Norman yoke'.

The central thesis in his *magnum opus*, *Labour in Irish history*, which he began to write in 1898, was a response to assumptions on the British left about socialism and nationalism. Historically, Irish workers took nationalism for granted; Connolly treated it as problematic, starting from a presumed dichotomy between socialism and nationalism, albeit to reconcile them. Ironically, it would have the effect of fixating socialists on the duality of the two. Socialists remember that Connolly turned the British left view of the Irish question inside out; they forget that it was a British view.

The contortions were compounded by a rigmarole about the real republican being a socialist and the real socialist being a republican (it depends on how one defines 'republican'), which Connolly

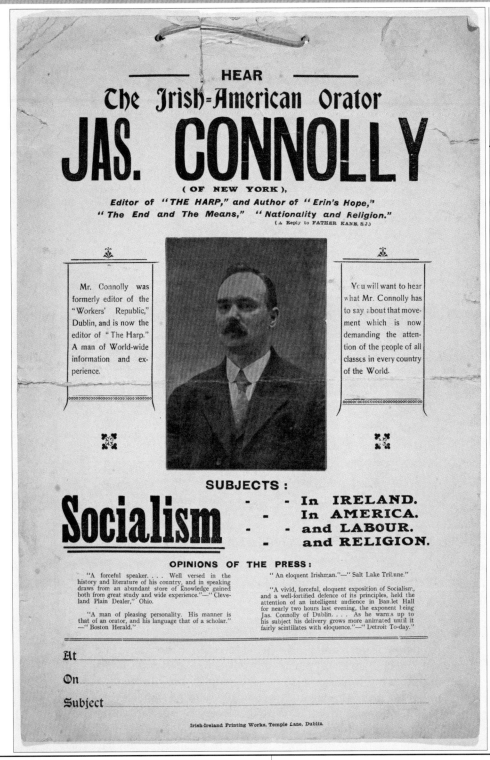

HEAR
The Irish=American Orator
JAS. CONNOLLY
(OF NEW YORK),
Editor of "THE HARP," and Author of "Erin's Hope,"
"The End and The Means," "Nationality and Religion."
(A Reply to FATHER KANE, S.J.)

Mr. Connolly was formerly editor of the "Workers' Republic," Dublin, and is now the editor of "The Harp." A man of World-wide information and experience.

You will want to hear what Mr. Connolly has to say about that movement which is now demanding the attention of the people of all classes in every country of the World.

SUBJECTS :
Socialism
- In IRELAND.
- In AMERICA.
- and LABOUR.
- and RELIGION.

OPINIONS OF THE PRESS :

"A forceful speaker. . . . Well versed in the history and literature of his country, and in speaking draws from an abundant store of knowledge gained both from great study and wide experience."—"Cleveland Plain Dealer," Ohio.

"A man of pleasing personality. His manner is that of an orator, and his language that of a scholar." —"Boston Herald."

"An eloquent Irishman."—"Salt Lake Tribune."

"A vivid, forceful, eloquent exposition of Socialism, and a well-fortified defence of its principles, held the attention of an intelligent audience in Bandlet Hall for nearly two hours last evening, the exponent being Jas. Connolly of Dublin. . . . As he warms up to his subject his delivery grows more animated until it fairly scintillates with eloquence."—"Detroit To-day."

At _____

On _____

Subject _____

Irish-Ireland Printing Works, Temple Lane, Dublin.

Left: A poster advertising an address by Connolly in the US. In time, the notorious fractiousness of the American far left made him increasingly homesick. The year 1907 was pivotal. In forming the Irish Socialist Federation in New York he confirmed his abiding interest in Ireland and began a drift from purist isolation towards the mainstream. (National Library of Ireland)

stone of Labour politics from 1830.[1]

Connolly would not make the same mistakes during his second stint in Ireland. By 1903 he was moving from the British Marxism of the SDF to the American syndicalism of Daniel De Leon's Socialist Labor Party, literally so when he emigrated to the United States. He was also tired of carrying the ISRP and, a firm feminist, was anxious to find a better world for his six daughters. The notorious fractiousness of the American far left made him increasingly homesick, however. The year 1907 was pivotal. In forming the Irish Socialist Federation in New York he confirmed his abiding interest in Ireland and began a drift from purist isolation towards the mainstream. In July 1910 he returned to Dublin to lead the Socialist Party of Ireland and give it a relatively moderate programme. In 1911 Larkin employed him as an organiser with the Irish Transport and General Workers Union (ITGWU), and in 1912 Connolly moved the motion at the ITUC in Clonmel that congress form a Labour Party. He opposed the suggestion that the ITUC be renamed the Labour Party lest it scare away the middle ground.

Connolly was now much better connected than in his ISRP days. He had also acquired an international reputation as a propagandist. His speeches read well, and he excelled at explaining the most complex aspects of socialism or syndicalism in clear and concise writing. In addition, unlike his general secretary, he was appreciated within the ITGWU as a fair-minded and competent administrator. Yet Larkin was the main man. Connolly was good at persuading those willing to sit and listen to him. Larkin could move the

deemed necessary to square his nationalism with his Marxism. In the process he exaggerated the radicalism of the republican tradition and the conservatism of the IPP, which enjoyed good relations with the British Labour Party and was far from the reactionary party that historians have made it out to be. Connolly's ideas would have been

more compelling and relevant if grounded on the Labour-nationalism of the early Irish trade unions and of Davitt. *Labour in Irish history* ends as trade unions emerge into legality, and 'the plan of the book … precluded any attempt to deal in detail with the growth, development, or decay of industry in Ireland', though this was the touch-

'In 1914 Connolly took the reins as acting general secretary of the ITGWU, commandant of the Citizen Army and editor of the Irish Worker. Three golden apples had fallen into his lap. How well he managed them is a matter of debate.'

masses. He was also Connolly's boss, and didn't let him forget it.

Curiously, they were polar opposites in personality and at one in policy. For decades, Labour and divers anti-nationalists, like Seán O'Casey, did their best to hide Larkin's republicanism, but Larkin differed from Connolly on the national question only in that he was more candid about his nationalism.

Both, too, were syndicalists, with identical views on industrial issues. It was Larkin's decision to leave the British-based National Union of Dock Labourers and found the ITGWU that powered the revival of an Irish Labour movement. And Larkin soon realised that nationalism was water to the mill of his contention that Irish workers needed Irish unions. This was the material basis of Labour's post-1909 socialist

republicanism, and it was Larkin who made it, just as he created the conditions for the formation of the Citizen Army and gave it a republican constitution and rationale after the Lockout.

One might also note that Connolly's line on Ulster, so often attributed to him exclusively, was typical of the British and Irish left of the period, and his prediction that partition would precipitate 'a carnival of reaction' was exceptional only in its eloquence.

Worn out after the Lockout, Larkin fled to New York in October 1914. Connolly took the reins as acting general secretary of the ITGWU, commandant of the Citizen Army and editor of the *Irish Worker*. Three golden apples had fallen into his lap. How well he managed them is a matter of debate. In the wake of the Lockout, the cash-strapped ITGWU was compelled to continue retrenching, and the early war years

were difficult times for unskilled unions. On the other hand, some workers, such as dockers, were finding that they could exploit their importance to the war effort to secure war bonuses.

Connolly's handling of dock disputes in Dublin and Waterford is open to criticism. Waterford dockers called him 'a master's man' for his refusal to sanction a strike. The Citizen Army remained small, though it was no easy feat to keep it going. And the very readable *Irish Worker* was suppressed by Dublin Castle and replaced with the more monochrome *Workers' Republic*.

One can be similarly ambivalent about the ultimate Connolly question: should he have gone out in Easter Week? From August 1914, he, and Larkin, had determined on a rising during the war. In what must have been a huge disappointment for Connolly and a devastating challenge to his claim that only the

Right: The Starry Plough, the flag of the Irish Citizen Army, the group founded in 1913 by James Connolly and Jack White. The flag was unveiled in 1914 and was flown over the Imperial Hotel by the ICA during the Rising. (National Museum of Ireland)

working class remained uncorrupted by British imperialism, the Irish, for the first time in their history, were backing Britain in a war. Labour complained of 'economic conscription'. Unskilled labourers, who made up 28% of men between the ages of 20 and 45, comprised 70–80% of recruits into the army's other ranks in wartime Ireland.[2]

But regardless of why people enlisted, the war was sealing bonds of blood and welfare between working-class families and the British state, and the legacy is still with us today. Many socialists believed that wartime regulations presaged the displacement of liberal capitalism by a new servility that would enslave the proletariat in the shackles of statism; the British left denounced conscription as 'Prussianism'. For an anti-imperialist, for a democrat, the case for a rising was strong, and if there was to be a rising the case for a Labour input was even stronger. Standing back would have done Labour no favours at all.

What is harder to square with socialism is Connolly's impatience for insurrection, oblivious to the evolving impact of the war. V.I. Lenin made probably the most astute observation on Easter Week when he said, in October 1916, that the Irish 'rose prematurely, when the European revolt of the proletariat had not yet matured'.[3] Should a socialist, republican or otherwise, not have seen that the world war was radicalising Europe and strengthening organised Labour? Or was it that war made the chronic acute, crystallising the options of shoot or salute, and tilting Connolly past a tipping point into near-unqualified nationalism?

Oddly, the great theorist had a simple prescription for revolution in Ireland: just do it, and do it now. If it works, then the time was right. If it doesn't work … better luck next time. He had urged Arthur Griffith, of all people, to lead a revolt during the Boer war—the Vietnam War of its day.

Leaving Labour behind him was the price Connolly had to pay for joining the action on Easter Monday 1916. But he had never been able to carry the mass of workers in the way Larkin had. With Connolly dead, and Larkin at odds with colleagues in one form or other from 1914, socialist republicanism

'Leaving Labour behind him was the price Connolly had to pay for joining the action on Easter Monday 1916. But he had never been able to carry the mass of workers in the way Larkin had.'

gradually abated as a force in the Labour movement under the passive leadership of Tom Johnson and T.J. O'Connell. What has never abated is the fascination of 'Connollyology', and the appeal of Connolly's ideas, clarity, courage, integrity and humanity. Worldwide, publications on Connolly exceeded 350 a decade ago. The latest figure stands at 1,000.

NOTES

1. James Connolly, *Labour in Irish history* (Dublin, 1956), p.121.
2. Thomas P. Dooley, *Irishmen or English soldiers? The times and world of a southern Catholic Irish man (1876–1916) enlisting in the British Army during the First World War* (Liverpool, 1995), p.8.
3. V.I. Lenin, *British Labour and British imperialism* (London, 1969), p.166.

●

Left: Nora Connolly, the second daughter of James, in Irish Volunteer uniform in Belfast. In the initial planning for the Rising she was sent to America with a secret message from her father. A lifelong Labour Party supporter, Nora published *Portrait of a rebel father* in 1935 and *James Connolly wrote for today—socialism* in 1978. *We shall rise again* appeared in 1981. She died that June, aged 87 or 88. (© Seamus Connolly, courtesy of Kilmainham Gaol, 17PC-I B52-06)

REBEL WOMEN

BY **MARY McAULIFFE**

One activist, 'Southwoman', wrote in the separatist newspaper *Irish Freedom* in late 1913 that there was nothing **'unwomanly in active patriotism'**.

Image: Members of the Irish Women Workers' Union, which was founded in 1911, on the steps of Liberty Hall about 1914. (NLI Keogh Collection)

"Freedom's Martyr's"
Members of the Irish Women Workers Union who suffered terms of imprisonment in the cause of Labour

The involvement of women was a culmination of many factors, notably their engagement with various nationalist, labour and feminist campaigns

ALLIES OR AUXILIARIES?

I n 1926 Countess Markievicz gave a 'little' account of those women who were involved in the Easter Rising. Some of the female participants were, as she recalled, 'enrolled like me in the Irish Citizen Army … some were members of Cumann na mBan, and others just women who were ready to die for Ireland'.

Of those women who were ready to 'die for Ireland', between 260 and 270 were active participants in the Rising. Markievicz herself, as a member of the Irish Citizen Army (ICA), was stationed at the St Stephen's Green/Royal College of Surgeons outpost, where she was second in command to Michael Mallin. The estimated total of 270

Helena Molony wrote, '*When we walked out that Easter Monday morning we felt, in a very real sense, that we were walking with Ireland into the sun*'.

women 'out' in Dublin, Galway, Enniscorthy and Ashbourne is obviously much smaller than the number of male rebels, estimated at about 2,500. Most of these women were members of either Cumann na mBan or the ICA.

By 1916, especially in Dublin, members of both organisations would have been conscious of the changing political landscape. In the weeks preceding the Rising, the febrile atmosphere in the city, with the preparations being undertaken in Liberty Hall (where women were making knapsacks, homemade bombs and learning first aid) and the constant route marches and parades in which they took part, indicated that rebellion was imminent and, perhaps, inevitable. The question is, however, whether the *direct* participation of women in such a rebellion was inevitable.

POLITICS
The involvement of women in the rebellion was a culmination of many factors, notably their engagement with the various nationalist, labour and feminist campaigns in the pre-

● Left: Dr Kathleen Lynn, one of several advanced nationalist women and suffragettes who were also members of the Irish Citizen Army. Dr Lynn delivered arms to the ICA brigade which attacked City Hall and, as Medical Officer and ranking officer, eventually surrendered the brigade. (National Library of Ireland)

ceding decades. From the Ladies Land League in 1881, through continuing suffrage campaigns, support for the Home Rule movement and involvement in cultural nationalist organisations, women had been engaged with all of the major political causes in Ireland. Where women were not allowed to join male-only groups they formed their own organisations. In 1900 Maud Gonne founded the feminist, separatist, cultural nationalist group Inghinidhe na hÉireann (Daughters of Ireland), one of the most important women's organisations of the early twentieth century. As historian Margaret Ward has noted, if Inghinidhe had not existed 'a whole generation of women would have never developed the self-confidence' which allowed them to hold their own in organisations that also included men.

The previous year, Hanna and Francis Sheehy Skeffington had helped found the Irish Women's Franchise League (IWFL). The IWFL represented a new generation of suffrage activists, a generation that had lost patience with the more moderate tactics of the older suffrage organisations. The IWFL was influenced by the militancy of the British Women's Social and Political Union, and was determined to push its ideology of 'Suffrage First, before all else'.

Despite some ideological divisions between activists about whether suffrage or nationalism should take priority, the women of Inghinidhe na hÉireann, Sinn Féin and the IWFL often found common ground in the many issues, especially social issues, in which they were engaged. Indeed, by 1912 Inghinidhe women were supportive of the campaign undertaken by the IWFL and others to have female suffrage included in the third Home Rule Bill.

Another cause that provided a unifying platform for advanced nationalist and feminist women was labour. Trade unionist and socialist James Connolly was a supporter of feminism, as he recognised the common ground between the struggles of labour and those of women. He was close to several activists, including Helena Molony,

Kathleen Lynn and Markievicz, who by 1911 were becoming more socialist in their thinking. In September 1911, when the Irish Women Workers' Union was founded, feminist Hanna Sheehy Skeffington shared a platform with Delia Larkin, Molony and Markievicz. After their activities in Liberty Hall during the 1913 Lockout, when female activists not only took roles considered traditionally feminine, such as providing food for striking workers, but also took part in strikes and pickets, several of these women became involved in the ICA. Many of the more socialist female activists preferred to join the ICA rather than any other militant nationalist organisation. It is telling that these women appreciated the atmosphere of equality that *they* felt prevailed in the ICA. Madeleine ffrench-Mullen told her friend Rosamund Jacob that 'there was absolutely no difference made between men and women in the Citizen Army'. And Sheehy Skeffington had referred to the 'slave-like status' of Cumann na mBan in relation to the Irish Volunteers.

Among the advanced nationalist women who were members of the ICA were Lynn, Markievicz, Molony, ffrench-Mullen, Marie Perolz and Nellie Gifford. As well as these 'élite' women, working-class women such as Rosie Hackett, Jinny

Shanahan, Bridget Brady, Martha Kelly, the Norgrove sisters and others, having been politicised through trade union activism and their experiences during the Lockout, joined the women's section of the ICA in 1914–15.

As advanced nationalism developed through 1913, in response to the passing of the third Home Rule Bill and the formation of the Ulster Volunteers, women were eager to get involved. The Irish Volunteers, founded in November 1913, indicated that 'there would be work for women to do' but showed no inclination to allow women into the ranks. Despite the misgivings of some men concerning the participation of women, one activist, 'Southwoman', wrote in the separatist newspaper *Irish Freedom* in late 1913 that there was nothing 'unwomanly in active patriotism'.

In the months after the formation of the Volunteers the idea of a separate nationalist organisation for women began to gather momentum, and on 2 April 1914 Cumann na

●

Below: Helena Molony (seated third from left, second row, beside Maud Gonne McBride) with members of Inghinidhe na hÉireann. Molony, an ICA officer and Abbey actor, wrote: 'When we walked out that Easter Monday morning we felt, in a very real sense, that we were walking with Ireland into the sun'. (National Library of Ireland)

mBan was launched at Wynn's Hotel in Dublin. The first debate among the activists, after the inaugural meeting, concerned the relationship of Cumann na mBan to the Irish Volunteers: auxiliaries or allies? The *Irish Citizen*, the suffrage newspaper, maintained that suffrage must always come first. That Cumann na mBan (many of whose members were also feminists) supported the ideal of nationalism offended feminist sensibilities. Cumann na mBan, however, defended its position; it saw itself as an ally of the Volunteers, an independent body determined to make its own decisions. Despite the setback of a split, which mirrored the split in the Irish Volunteers occasioned by John Redmond's Woodenbridge speech in support of the war effort in September 1914, Cumann na mBan was, by the end of 1915, the largest women's nationalist organisation in the country.

PREPARATION AND PARTICIPATION

In the months leading up to the Rising, women from both the ICA and Cumann na mBan were engaged in preparations. Margaret 'Loo' Kennedy, a member of the Inghinidhe branch of Cumann na mBan, described their training: 'In Camden Street we were trained and exercised in drill, figure marching, stretcher-drill, signalling and rifle practice … we also went on route marches regularly … we had two instructors from the Fianna for drill, signalling and rifle practice'.

The general thinking among the Irish Volunteers, however, was that this was not suitable activity for women. Lily O'Brennan, in her statement to the Advisory Committee of the Pensions Board in 1935, responded to the question as to the 'object of rifle practices': 'It was mostly to learn how to clean a rifle. The original idea was that we might be alongside the men, and if a

Volunteer got wounded we might be able to empty the rifle.'

In Liberty Hall, in the weeks before Easter Sunday, ICA women were making bandages, collecting cans to make bombs, studying first aid with Dr Lynn and making first aid outfits, and taking messages to and from the leaders. Cumann na mBan women like Brigid Foley or Marie Perolz were sent by Pearse, Mac Diarmada and other planners of the Rising on longer trips down the country, taking messages to and from Volunteer leaders in Cork, Tralee, Waterford, Galway and Belfast. As the rebellion began, the trusted activist Rosie Hackett carried messages from Connolly to the printers of the Proclamation.

Nevertheless, while a number of the more well-connected and politically engaged women may have suspected or known that something was soon to happen, for most women the Rising came as a surprise. Despite this, once the fighting began, women willingly joined in. As Helena Molony wrote, 'When we walked out that Easter Monday morning we felt, in a very real sense, that we were walking with Ireland into the sun'.

Because of the confusion caused by Eoin MacNeill's countermanding order, only one branch of Cumann na mBan in Dublin, the Inghinidhe branch, was effectively mobilised. These women spent Easter Week in the Marrowbone Lane outpost under Captain Rose McNamara. They were

Right: Nurse Elizabeth O'Farrell left 16 Moore Street to tell the British that the GPO garrison would surrender. She later brought Pearse's surrender order to the other garrisons. (Donna Cooney)

attached to the 4th Battalion of the Dublin Brigade of the Irish Volunteers, under the command of Éamonn Ceannt. Members of the Central, Fairview and Colmcille branches of Cumann na mBan made their way individually or in groups to outposts at the GPO, St Stephen's Green and the Four Courts, while 29 women members of the ICA also participated, mainly at City Hall and St Stephen's Green/Royal College of Surgeons. For the most part these women operated as helpers, nurses and cooks, although a few, such as Margaret Skinnider, stationed with Mallin and Markievicz at the Royal College of Surgeons, took part in the fighting.

The most vital work undertaken by women was the carrying of dispatches between the commandants in the various outposts. Because they were not generally in uniform (other than some in Red Cross uniforms) and usually not under suspicion by the British soldiers manning the barricades, the women couriers could make their way through a city under increasing bombardment. Although the work was dangerous, the women took a quiet pride in this contribution. Cumann na mBan Central branch members and couriers Máire Carron and Nellie Ennis felt that they had done no more than their expected duty.

CONCLUSION

As the Rising came to its conclusion, the commandants at the outposts requested that the women make their escape; some acquiesced, while others, like the women at Marrowbone Lane, refused, insisting that 'they were part of the rebel contingent and were surrendering with the rest'. In all, 77 women were arrested and imprisoned in the immediate aftermath of the Rising, although most would be released within ten days.

The role of women in the Rising has long been a subject for debate. Obviously women were not among the central planners of the Rising, but neither did they force themselves on male revolutionaries reluctant to accept women alongside them in the fight. Even those women who were members of the ICA generally took on conventional feminine roles. As a woman in a command position, an aristocrat by birth and a long-time activist, socialist, nationalist and feminist, Countess Markievicz is somewhat of an outlier when it comes to understanding the participation of women in the Rising. Unlike Markievicz, many of the female rebels were young, unmarried, working-class or lower middle-class, and most had been activists for only a few years beforehand.

Despite their growing politicisation through feminism, nationalism and trade unionism, involvement in violent revolution was an extraordinary step for women conditioned by society to accept the primacy of the domestic role. Contemporary newspaper reports echo the general disbelief at the actions of these women. The *Irish Examiner* was aghast that 'amongst the prisoners taken away … [were] young women in male attire … bearing arms in the streets against British soldiers'.

As historians have noted, it is not the number of women who fought in the Rising (or, indeed, the roles they performed) that is important but that they were there at all. Whether as cooks, nurses, couriers or snipers, they carried out their duties in a very public context as combatants in a military campaign for Irish freedom. Most of the female rebels did not, in fact, bear arms or wear male clothing, but their radicalisation in such a violent revolution became reflected in the increasingly feminist and militant standpoint of Cumann na mBan in the post-Rising years. By 1917 their demands included the 'arming and equipping of the men *and women* of Ireland' and a commitment to 'follow the policy of the Republican Proclamation of 1916 by seeing that women take up their proper position in the life of the nation'. Nothing less than full and equal citizenship, as promised in the Proclamation, was to be the result of their contribution to revolution.

Despite the traumas suffered during the fight, most of these women continued their activism

after the Rising. The contribution of women to the reorganisation of Cumann na mBan and, indeed, of the Irish Volunteers, to the nationalist propaganda campaigns and fundraising, and to keeping the revolutionary flame burning would become more vital in the months and years ahead.

Further reading

L. Gillis, *Women of the Irish Revolution: a photographic history* (Cork, 2013).

C. McCarthy, *Cumann na mBan and the Irish Revolution* (Cork, 2009).

S. Pašeta, *Irish nationalist women 1900–1918* (Cambridge, 2013).

M. Ward, *Unmanageable revolutionaries: women and Irish nationalism* (Dublin, 1996).

●

Above: Dr Kathleen Lynn with Madeleine ffrench-Mullen. ICA member ffrench-Mullen, who was with the St Stephen's Green garrison, had told her friend Rosamund Jacob that 'there was absolutely no difference made between men and women in the Citizen Army'. (National Library of Ireland)

CROWN FORCES

BRITISH

BY **DEREK MOLYNEUX & DARREN KELLY**

SOLDIERS

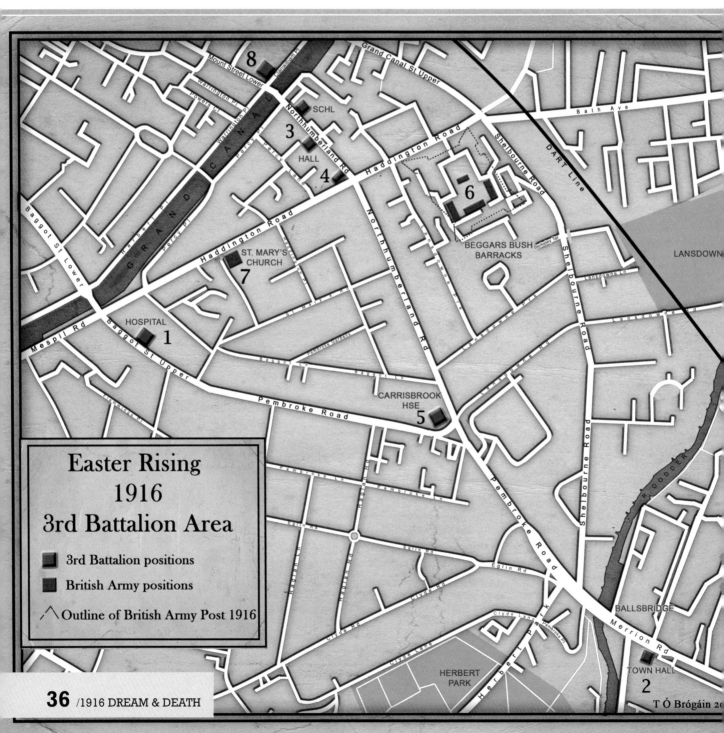

Mount Street Lower

8

Clanwilliam Pl

Grand Canal St Upper

Bath Ave

Warrington Pl

SCHL

Northumberland Rd

Haddington Road

DART Line

Percy Pl

Percy La

3

HALL

Shelbourne Road

4

6

Baggot St Lower

GRAND CANAL

BEGGARS BUSH
BARRACKS

Berkeley Ter

LANSDOWN

Haddington Road

ST. MARY'S
CHURCH

7

Northumberland Rd

Shelbourne Road

Lansdowne Rd

Mespil Rd

HOSPITAL

Baggot St Upper

1

Pembroke Gardens

Baggot La

Shelbourne Road

Pembroke Road

CARRISBROOK
HSE

5

R. DODDER

Easter Rising
1916
3rd Battalion Area

■ 3rd Battalion positions

■ British Army positions

∧ Outline of British Army Post 1916

Pembroke Road

Eglin Rd

BALLSBRIDGE

Merrion Rd

HERBERT
PARK

TOWN HALL

2

T Ó Brógáin 20

Hundreds of inexperienced Sherwood Foresters were marched blindly into the bloodiest battle of the week

SLAUGHTER AT MOUNT STREET

The ranks of the 2/7th Sherwood Foresters reached the southern section of Northumberland Road shortly after mid-day on Wednesday 26 April. C Company took point position. Many of its 200 young recruits, each carrying full packs, held their rifles with trembling hands. Their perspiring faces turned from side to side as they scanned the road's three-storey red-brick houses. As gunfire rang out in the distance, their trepidation increased with each advancing step. But hundreds of boots tramping in step to their rear accompanied by the shouts of sergeants compelled them to suppress their fear.

●

Left: The area of operations of the Irish Volunteers, 3rd Battalion. (Tomás Ó Brogáin)

1. 16–18 Baggot Street Upper—Royal City of Dublin Hospital, commonly called Baggot Street Hospital. Used to treat British and Irish casualties of the Rising.
2. Merrion Road, Ballsbridge—Pembroke/Ballsbridge Town Hall. Éamon de Valera was held here after the Rising.
3. 1–5 Northumberland Road—St Stephen's Schoolhouse and Parochial Hall. Held by the Volunteers, right at Mount Street Bridge.
4. 25 Northumberland Road, at the corner of Haddington Road. Held by two Volunteers, whose fire inflicted great damage on the British advancing on Mount Street Bridge.
5. 122–124 Pembroke Road, at Northumberland Road. Carrisbrook House was taken early by the Volunteers; it was quickly abandoned.
6. Shelbourne Road—Beggar's Bush Barracks. The main training depot for the British army, it was very lightly garrisoned.
7. Haddington Road—St Mary's Church. The British had snipers in the bell-tower here.
8. 1–2 Clanwilliam Place—Clanwilliam House. Seven Volunteers held this key post; three were killed and four survived.

The British Army's 178th Infantry Brigade, under Brigadier Colonel Maconchy, had landed at Kingstown by 6.00 that morning. The brigade was formed of four battalions of Sherwood Foresters, each consisting of approximately 800 men from the English east midlands. To advance and retake the city, the brigade was divided into two formations. The first consisted of the 2/5th and 2/6th battalions, who marched inland through Stillorgan and Donnybrook towards the city, while the 2/7th and 2/8th battalions followed the coast road through Blackrock and eventually Ballsbridge, heading for Trinity College.

C Company stopped momentarily at the junction of St Mary's Road, as A, B and D Companies took supporting positions, amid reports that they were about to enter the danger zone. Then several barked orders had C Company's four platoons, each of 50 soldiers, advancing again; their objective was St Stephen's Schoolhouse, roughly 300m to their front and right. As the company moved forward its platoons adopted box formations, a standard procedure in built-up areas.

As the soldiers reached the junction with Haddington Road the rebels suddenly let loose on them. The crossroads instantly became a scene of carnage. Semi-automatic fire smashed into the ranks of troops. Order disintegrated. Men screamed as they were hit. Some dropped to the cobblestones seeking cover, but there seemed no escape. Shouts for medics followed. Captain Dietrichsen, the Battalion Adjutant, was one of the first shot.

Captain Pragnell ordered a charge. The company's forward sec-tions charged at the corner house to their front and left, No. 25 Northumberland Road, from where the rebel fire emanated. But the men were shot down on its steps by concentrated fire from Clanwilliam Terrace to their west. The survivors scurried away.

Colonel Fane, the 2/7th Battalion commander, reacted quickly. He ordered Major Hanson to take three of B Company's platoons and advance along Haddington Road to outflank the enemy positions. C Company would provide cover.

Soon the corner house was subjected to an avalanche of bullets. B Company then rushed forward, losing several men at the crossroads before making their left turn. Then the rate of enemy fire increased. Men fell, their hands clutching at wounds. A nearby wall was soon stained red, while the gaps between the road's cobblestones became wet as wounds haemorrhaged profusely. Roughly twenty men lay strewn on the road.

Hanson's manoeuvre succeeded and he took Baggot Street Bridge. Leaving a single platoon to secure it, he ordered the remaining two platoons to turn north and advance into Percy Place, with the Grand Canal to their left, in an attempt to assault the Schoolhouse. The infantrymen pushed forward cautiously, until shots reported from beyond the canal. Some rushed for the nearby houses to their right as rounds smashed into the façades. More soldiers fell to the fire. With no way out, the remaining troops scrambled for cover along the canal's coping stones, which stood

> Many soldiers were hit as they crawled, forcing their horrified comrades to struggle over their bodies to press on.

Above: British soldiers on Northumberland Road during a lull in the fighting. (UCD Archives)

no more than 12in. and 18in. high.

Back on Northumberland Road, most of the Sherwood Foresters had taken cover behind the many flights of steps in the surrounding gardens. After a period of regrouping, a trench-whistle sounded, prompting 60 terrified infantrymen to charge along the road. More collapsed under the fire from No. 25 as a section peeled away to assault its steps again, only to suffer the same fate as their comrades earlier. As the remainder pressed on, they were hit by a broadside fusillade from the Parochial Hall on their left flank. Another volley followed, and was succeeded by a wall of shot from ahead of the soldiers. The slaughter was appalling. Only a dozen made it to the Schoolhouse. Once through its iron gates, however, there was little shelter for the now leaderless troops. Rebels in Clanwilliam House began to pick off the remaining men.

The same rebels now trained their guns on the troops from B Company huddling next to the canal in Percy Place. Soon Major Hanson became a casualty, prompting a sergeant to summon several sections for a frontal assault on the Schoolhouse. The result was inevitable. A wall of fire greeted them from Clanwilliam House and from elevated positions to the soldiers' front in Boland's Mills, 400m to the east.

Shortly before 2pm, Colonel Fane ordered Captain Wright of A Company to take his men and outflank the enemy position from its eastern side. The captain soon set off along Shelbourne Road, until heavy fire from enemy positions to his front and right drove him back.

An hour later Colonel Fane realised that his options were running out. A runner returned from battalion headquarters with instructions on where to procure machine-guns and explosives. Meanwhile, the colonel formulated a new plan. He ordered D Company, under Captain Cooper,

to occupy houses opposite No. 25. Soon the air resounded again with the high-pitched cracks of Enfield rifles. Unfortunately for the ragged remainder of C Company, who had been ordered to reinforce B Company, the same air also rang again with the echoes of rebel weapons. The earlier carnage was repeated. The wide road junction was now littered with dead and wounded men. Those who had survived the onslaught scrambled into Percy Lane, with orders to press on and provide support to their hard-pressed comrades from B Company in Percy Place. As they emerged from the laneway more of them fell to the rebel weapons. Captain Pragnell was hit.

After a time a prolonged lull developed. The still air was filled with pitiful groans. The Sherwood Foresters now completely filled the southern section of Northumberland Road, a khaki mass pushing relentlessly on. Infantrymen converged in several lines on the ground sliding forward, developing into great caterpillar formations. An eerie silence hung in the air, until without warning the firing resumed.

As the enemy rifles shooting from roughly 300m away zeroed in, it seemed impossible for them to miss a target. Many soldiers were hit as they crawled, forcing their horrified comrades to struggle over their bodies to press on. Recognising this, their junior officers blew their whistles; the blasts were followed by barked commands from the NCOs, which propelled men to their feet to rush forward into a storm of bullets. Wave after wave followed, to meet the same fate. Every time a whistle blew, another group of young men charged side by side and fell under the lethal hail. The Sherwood Foresters were being slaughtered.

Teams of doctors and nurses from the nearby Sir Patrick Dun's hospital began to arrive and brave the fire from both sides. Their overgarments quickly resembled the aprons of abattoir workers as they worked in the impromptu ceasefire that followed their sudden appearance on the battlefield. They weren't the only non-combatants to make

an appearance. Scores of civilians had formed a crescent close to Love Lane on Lower Mount Street, keen not to miss out on the murderous matinée.

Soon the ceasefire was abandoned. As the medics scrambled for cover, a loud cry of 'Good old Notts' heralded several more charges, but it was useless. Men slipped on the blood of their fallen comrades while the air whistled with rounds.

After several further assaults, a machine-gun began to bark loudly in the afternoon air. Puffs of smoke billowed from the bell-tower of St Mary's Church on Haddington Road, as the Vickers gun placed there spewed fire at the rebel position across the canal. Meanwhile, the British regimental commander, Colonel Maconchy, ordered the 2/8th Battalion to send a single company on an outflanking manoeuvre to the

Above: Captain Frederick Christian Dietrichsen was among the Sherwoods killed at Mount Street. Pictured here with a group of officers in 1915, he is third from the right in the row of seated men. From Nottingham, he was a barrister before he joined the British army, and his wife was a Mitchell from Dublin. She and their two young daughters had gone to Dublin for safety to escape the Zeppelin raids. They were actually in Blackrock waving flags on the pavement when Captain Dietrichsen marched the Sherwoods through. 'His fellow officers saw Dietrichsen drop out of the column and fling his arms around the children. It was a joyful scene with no hint of the tragedy to come'—Max Caulfield, *The Easter Rebellion*. (Picture from *Illustrated War News*, 20 October 1915)

east along Grand Canal Street. This decision was overruled, however, in the course of a telephone call to the overall British commander, Brigadier General Lowe, and the slaughter continued.

Maconchy went forward from his headquarters to assess the situation. He was informed by Colonel Fane, himself now wounded, that the remaining men of the 2/7th and the entire 2/8th Battalion would be required to overwhelm the enemy. Lieutenant Colonel Oates, in command of the 2/8th, was given his orders: he was to overrun the Schoolhouse 'at all costs'.

At 5pm, however, the arrival of reinforcements with explosives, under Captain Jeffaires of the Elm Park Bombing School, heralded the imminent end of No. 25 as a defensive position. A section of troops braved the fire from its windows and fixed gun-cotton to its front door, which soon succumbed to a deafening blast. Troops then stormed in, but quickly scrambled back outside as the cracks of pistol fire resounded from within. Several more had been shot down in its barricaded hallway. Soon, soldiers rushed into the house from its rear, and within minutes the first rebel stronghold in the area had fallen. A solitary rebel lay dead inside.

The next move that the Sherwood Foresters made on Northumberland Road was to assault the Parochial Hall, 100 yards away to

their left in a recess back from the road. Relays of sections launched themselves forward, shouting and hurling hand grenades towards its windows. They braved a storm of fire from the hall itself and from Clanwilliam House, losing several men, but quickly overwhelmed the position. From here, their sights immediately fell once again upon the Schoolhouse.

At 6.30pm, the infantrymen from B Company 2/8th, under the command of Lieutenant Daffen, opened up with a broadside of fire that ripped into the Schoolhouse. They then made their assault, but were driven to ground by the fire from across the canal. Captain Quibell now ordered A Company to open up from the gardens on the eastern side of the road to cover them, while Lieutenant Foster from the 2/7th seized his opportunity. He stormed the Schoolhouse with a small detachment and forced entry, only to find the position devoid of the enemy. They were confronted instead with the bodies of the school's caretaker and his wife.

Soon Lieutenant Foster was joined by Captain Cooper, who with the remaining men of D Company 2/7th had approached the Schoolhouse from the rear of the nearby houses. The captain ordered them to take positions behind a 4ft wall next to the canal, and to open fire on the enemy positions on its far side. A nearby advertising hoarding was soon shot to pieces by the return fire of the insurgents, whose efforts were augmented by their comrades shooting from diagonally across the canal in Robert's Builder's Yard, and from further away in Boland's Mills. Cooper needed to make his move. Men were falling all around.

Lieutenant Daffen blew his whistle, prompting his company to rush across the bridge. He was the first to die. His company repeatedly charged, into defilading fire from their front in Clanwilliam House and enfilading fire from the railway line and workshops 300m to their right. All of their officers were hit. Soon their bodies became stacked in piles on the bridge, prompting the doc-

tors and nurses to once again brave the fire and tend to the wounded.

Captain Cursham now moved forward with C Company to take up the attack, while A Company took up supporting positions around the bridge. Whistles again signalled several more charges. By now the writing was on the wall for the stubborn rebel position. Men rushed the railings of Clanwilliam House hurling grenades, one with such venom that it bounced from the building's second floor only to fall and explode next to his head. His shattered body crumpled like a sack in the front garden.

Heavy fire sliced into the attacking troops from their right as they swarmed around the house. Both Captain Quibell, leading the assault, and Captain Cursham were hit. The fire, however, had begun to

dissipate from the upper rooms, suggesting that the end was at hand. Smoke began to billow from its broken windows. Lieutenant Foster, having quickly taken command, threw a grenade through a side window facing Lower Mount Street, and quickly followed the deafening blast which displaced its fortifications by scrambling inside. A dozen men quickly followed.

Acrid smoke soon filled the house. Small fires were breaking out in every room. Foster assaulted what was left of the staircase, and through the thick smoke spotted the silhouette of what he thought was a rebel at a front window. He pulled the pin on a grenade, counted for a couple of seconds and hurled the bomb inside. He wrenched the door closed and crouched behind the nearby

wall. As soon as the ensuing blast shook the house, he charged inside, pointing his revolver. Two men lay dead on the floor. Nearby was the remainder of a mannequin, riddled with bullets, having fallen from the window.

Finding only three dead men, the soldiers scrambled outside once again, keen to escape the rapidly spreading flames. The house soon became an inferno. As the daylight turned to dusk they regrouped on the street, where officers were shouting at stupefied men to remain in cover. Enemy fire was still coming from the railway line to their east.

As night closed in, the Sherwood Foresters took stock. Dead and wounded infantrymen were strewn about the entire area. Civilians looked on in disbelief. When the area had been secured, Colonel Maconchy rode to the scene on horseback, cheered on by tremendously relieved locals. His men did not feel like cheering. Both battalions between them had suffered 234 casualties, including eighteen officers. They had found only four enemy dead, and captured another four, from a fight that had lasted nine hours.

Further reading

D. Molyneux & D. Kelly, *When the clock struck in 1916: close-quarter combat in the Easter Rising* (Cork, 2015).

W.C. Oates, *The Sherwood Foresters in the Great War 1914–1918. The 2/8th Battalion* (Nottingham, 1920).

Various authors, *'The Robin Hoods': 1/7th, 2/7th, & 3/7th Battns. Sherwood Foresters 1914–1918* (Nottingham, 1921).

●

Above left: No. 25 Northumberland Road, at the north-west corner with Haddington Road, after the battle. The house had been 'donated' to the rebels by a sympathiser. (National Library of Ireland)

●

Left: The first to die at Mount Street were a group of reserve volunteer soldiers, the 'Gorgeous Wrecks', as they were nicknamed in Dublin on account of their age and the inscription on their tunics (Georgius Rex). While returning from a routine march in the Dublin foothills, they stumbled upon the rebels and four were killed before they reached safety at Beggar's Bush Barracks.

POLICEMEN

BY **BARTLE FAULKNER**

Image: Three members of the unarmed Dublin Metropolitan Police in full uniform in the yard of Dublin Castle. (National Library of Ireland)

Seventeen members of the DMP or RIC were killed while trying to keep the peace

SIMPLY DOING THEIR DUTY

Of the 485 people killed in the 1916 Rising, 54% were civilians caught up in the exchanges between the British forces and the rebels. Many are well-known, even iconic figures, with various monuments to their memory.

But there is a small group of people, 4% of those who died during the rebellion, who have been forgotten. This small group consists of seventeen policemen—three from the Dublin Metropolitan Police and fourteen from the Royal Irish Constabulary—killed in their efforts to keep the peace in their own land. For the record, they are listed below.

DMP:
- Constable James O'Brien, shot dead at the upper gate of the Castle Yard on Easter Monday.
- Constable Michael Lahiff, shot dead on St Stephen's Green the same day.

- Constable William Frith, shot at Store Street Police Station on 27 April.

RIC:
The following eight members were killed in the Battle of Ashbourne on 28 April:
- County Inspector Alexander Gray,
- District Inspector Harry Smyth,
- Sergeant John Shanagher,
- Sergeant John Young,
- Constable James Hickey,
- Constable James Gormley,
- Constable Richard McHale,
- Constable James Cleary.

- On 26 April, two RIC men, Sergeant Thomas O'Rourke and Constable John Hurley, were killed in Monour, Co. Tipperary.
- Constable Christopher Miller was shot and mortally wounded at the South Dublin Union on 27 April.
- Head Constable William Rowe was shot dead in Castlelyons, Co. Cork, on 2 May.

ROYAL IRISH CONSTABULARY
Most of Ireland's regional police forces had been consolidated in 1836, creating an Irish Constabulary. This constabulary had absorbed the police forces of Belfast and Derry in 1865 and 1870 and was responsible thereafter for the whole island outside of Dublin, which had its own Metropolitan Police. This body finally became the Royal Irish Constabulary as a reward for its part in crushing the uprising of 1867.

The RIC comprised about 10,000 men, all of them Irish and most of them Catholic. By 1916 the RIC had become a domesticated

Above left: Constable James O'Brien of the DMP, believed to be the first fatality of the Rising. The 48-year-old was on regular duty at the upper gate of the Castle Yard. At approximately noon on Monday a company of the Irish Citizen Army led by Captain Seán Connolly marched up to the gate. Constable O'Brien approached and was shot in the head by Connolly. It was described as an 'impetuous' shooting. (Courtesy of Kilmainham Gaol Museum—KMGLM 2015.0675)

civil police force. There was little ordinary crime in Ireland, and as a result the police had been assigned a wide variety of civil service duties. They acted as inspectors of weights and measures, collected censuses or compiled annual statistics of tillage and livestock, among many other duties.

The RIC was an armed force, but not since the agrarian disputes of the early 1880s did individual members carry their firearms. Thus, when County Inspector Alexander Gray gathered 50 of his men in Slane on the morning of 28 April to assist their colleagues who were under siege at Ashbourne barracks, he was keenly aware of their lack of experience in the use of firearms.

Thomas Ashe was Commandant of the Fifth Battalion of the Irish Volunteers, with Lieutenant Richard Mulcahy as his deputy. The battalion was 120 strong, but owing to Eoin McNeill's countermanding order only 60 turned out near Swords on Easter Monday. By Tuesday that figure was reduced to 40, as Commandant James Connolly ordered that twenty men should be sent to support the garrison in the GPO.

For the remainder of the week they travelled around north County Dublin by bicycle, raiding RIC stations, including Swords, Donabate and Garristown. Guns and ammunition were seized and many RIC stations had to be evacuated. Early on Friday 28 April, 40 men in three sections set out from their overnight camp in Garristown to make their way to Batterstown to blow up the railway line. As the Volunteer scouting party was passing through Ashbourne, however, they encountered three fully armed policemen cycling on the main road. Two of the policemen dropped their guns and ran off, but Sergeant Brady, who recognised one of the Volunteers as

Gerry Golden, stood his ground. Golden tried to shoot him, but his gun jammed.

Eventually Sergeant Brady was captured and was forced by Commandant Ashe to walk with a white flag up to Ashbourne police station and order the men inside to surrender. This approach did not work, and it was only after a number of grenades were thrown at the station that the men inside shouted, 'We surrender'.

But just as Ashe and Mulcahy were moving forward to take the surrender, a convoy of fifteen cars led by County Inspector Gray approached Rath Cross, a few

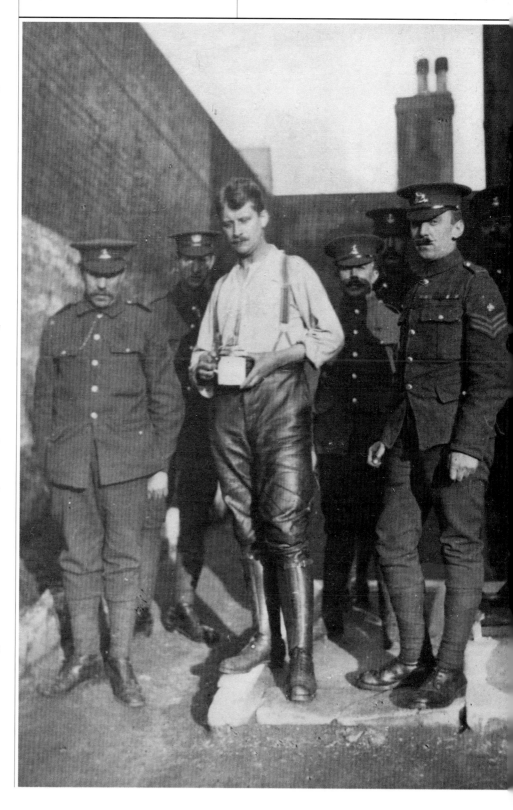

Right: Thomas Ashe surrounded by British soldiers, possibly in Kilmainham Gaol, after the battle of Ashbourne, Co. Meath. Ashe was commandant of the Fifth Battalion of the Irish Volunteers, with Lieutenant Richard Mulcahy as his deputy. (NLI)

Above: Irish Volunteers (inc. ICA) fire a volley over the grave of Thomas Ashe at his funeral in Glasnevin Cemetery in 1917. Ashe died after being force-fed while on hunger strike. (National Library of Ireland)

hundred yards from the station. When he saw these reinforcements Ashe ordered his men to retreat, but Mulcahy intervened, believing that they had surprised the RIC as much as they themselves had been surprised. He instructed his men behind the barracks to attack the new arrivals on their left flank while the others mounted the bank on the other side.

As a result, deadly fire was opened on the police from both sides, and from the outset they were required to take cover under the cars and in the surrounding ditches. Inspector Gray received a wound to the hand and Sergeant Shanagher was shot through the heart as he was leaving the car. He fell into the ditch in a sitting position and was found that way later.

The battle continued throughout the afternoon, with Gray refusing to surrender. It wasn't until he had been wounded in both hands and in the body and the Volunteers had surrounded them that the RIC surrendered. As a result of the battle, seventeen constables were wounded and one county inspector, one district inspector, two sergeants and four constables were shot dead. These men were all from local barracks in County Meath: Navan, Killyon, Longwood, Kells, Crossakiel and Moynalty. Two Volunteers were mortally wounded, both north Dublin men: John Crennigan and Thomas Rafferty.

County Inspector Gray is buried in Esker Cemetery, Lucan; District Inspector Harry Smyth is buried in Ardbraccan, Co. Meath; Sergeant John Shanagher is buried in Killina Cemetery, Co. Roscommon; and Sergeant John Young and Constables James Hickey, James Gormley and Richard McHale are all buried in St Mary's Cemetery in Navan.

On Easter Monday, at Castlebellingham, Co. Louth, Constable Charles McGee was shot dead by Irish Volunteers from Dundalk under the command of Denis Hannigan. The Volunteers, who were making their way by cavalcade to meet Ashe's men, had stopped for provisions. They had taken two local RIC men captive when McGee, from nearby

Below: Richard Mulcahy, who went on to serve as Minister for Defence during the Civil War. (National Library of Ireland)

Gilberstown barracks, cycled into the village. The circumstances of his shooting are unclear. He died in the Louth County Hospital that evening. In June four Dundalk men were court-martialled in relation to his death. One of those men was Seán McEntee, an electrical engineer from Belfast working in Dundalk and a captain in the local Volunteers. McEntee was convicted and sentenced to penal servitude for life, but was released from prison one year later in June 1917. Constable McGee was 24 and came from Inisbofin, Co. Donegal. He is buried in Gortahork Cemetery in his native county.

Two days later a group of RIC men left Eglinton Street barracks in Galway under the command of Inspector Heard. Their mission was to patrol the Claregalway/Castlegar area, where barracks were under threat from Volunteers under the overall command of Liam Mellows. When Inspector Heard and his men had reached Carnmore, near Oranmore, they were ambushed by Volunteers who were situated behind stone walls on each side of the road. During this encounter Constable Patrick Whelan was shot dead. It is believed that Whelan knew his attackers and was endeavouring to talk to them when he was shot. Whelan was a native of Kilkenny and worked as a farmer before he joined the RIC in 1908. After a large funeral, he was buried in the New Cemetery in Bohermore in Galway City.

On 28 April, in Monour, Co. Tipperary, Sergeant Thomas O'Rourke and Constable John Hurley, both attached to the RIC barracks at Lisvernane in the Glen of Aherlow, went to a house in search of local Volunteer officer Michael O'Callaghan. He had been accused of firing shots indiscriminately in Tipperary town the evening before and hitting a boy called Ryan in the leg. The officers entered the house of Peter Hennessy, a cousin of O'Callaghan. The latter was in the house and without warning fired point-blank at Sergeant O'Rourke. He then pursued

Constable Hurley out the door and shot him before escaping.

Sergeant O'Rourke was buried in Clonbeg, near the Glen, where, as a serving policeman, he was very popular. Constable Hurley was brought home to Castletownbere for burial. Michael O'Callaghan left Ireland, eventually making his way to New York. He was arrested there on a separate criminal damage charge and the British authorities made every effort to have him extradited for the murder of two policemen. The extradition proceedings were eventually dropped.

On the first day of the Rising, Commandant Éamonn Ceannt of the Fourth Battalion of the Irish Volunteers took over the South Dublin Union, now the site of St James's Hospital. The British tried to oust Ceannt's troops but failed and had to look for reinforcements. On Thursday, 30 soldiers and twenty RIC men who were undergoing a British army NCO training course in nearby Portobello barracks were marching to the Phoenix Park when they were diverted to the South Dublin Union. Constable Christopher Miller was part of that company. Late that evening, Ceannt, with his badly wounded second-in-command Cathal Brugha and other Volunteers, were held up in the Nurses' Home. They could hear the enemy, now under the command of Sir Francis Vane of the Royal Munster Fusiliers, trying to break down the barricaded front door. The gunfire was so intense that the rooms were filled with plaster dust. Ceannt and Volunteer Peader Doyle ran to the front door and made strenuous efforts to push it closed. Ceannt stuck his automatic pistol through the gap in the door and squeezed the trigger, shooting dead Constable Miller, who was pushing on the other side. Constable Miller is buried in Bully's Acre in the Royal Hospital, Kilmainham. He was from County Limerick, and after joining the RIC in 1908 he served in Kerry, Armagh and Belfast.

The final RIC officer to die that week was Head Constable William

IRISH REBELLION, MAY, 1916.

SEAN CONNOLLY,
(Irish Republican Army),
Killed in Action at City Hall, Dublin, Easter Monday, 1916.

Rowe from Fermoy, shot dead on 2 May in Castlelyons. Rowe led an RIC party to the home of the Kent family, known as 'Bunnard'. With two sergeants and five constables, they surrounded the house, which was believed to contain firearms. It was reported that when Rowe and Sergeant Calbeck knocked on the back door, a defiant 'No surrender' was shouted from the kitchen.

Inside the house were the four Kent brothers—Tom, William, David and Dick—with their 86-year-old mother. A shot was fired from the house and Rowe and his men retreated behind a low wall. Several more shots rang out and Rowe was hit and fell to the ground. The exchange of fire continued and David Kent was wounded. Soon army reinforcements arrived and the Kents decided to surrender. In the course of the arrest, Richard Kent attempted to escape but was fired

●

Above: The memorial postcard for Seán Connolly. After Connolly had shot Constable O'Brien, the ICA group retreated to the City Hall, where Connolly, while on the roof, was shot dead by a sniper. (NLI)

upon by the army and fell badly wounded. He died a few days later. Thomas Kent was subsequently court-martialled and sentenced to death. On 9 May he was executed by a firing squad of Scottish Borderers. Head Constable Rowe left a widow and five children. He is buried in Castlehyde graveyard in Fermoy.

DUBLIN METROPOLITAN POLICE

The Easter Rising was predominantly a Dublin event. That thirteen of the seventeen policemen killed were from outside the Dublin area is surprising. It is explained in some way by the fact that the DMP, an unarmed force, were withdrawn from the streets on Monday evening. By 1pm on that day, however, two of their members lay dead.

Constable James O'Brien (48) was on regular duty at the upper gate of the Castle Yard (Cork Hill). He was a well-known figure at that location and would often be seen saluting nurses going in and out of the Red Cross Hospital, which was based in Dublin Castle. At approximately noon, a company of the Irish Citizen Army under the leadership of Captain Seán Connolly marched up to the Cork Hill Gate. Constable O'Brien approached them and within seconds he had been shot in the head by Connolly. It was described as an 'impetuous' shooting. Intentional or not, O'Brien lay dead. Connolly and his troops withdrew to the City Hall, where a short time later Connolly himself was shot on the roof by a sniper. After Requiem Mass in Mount Argus, Constable O'Brien's remains were taken by train and interred in Glin, Co. Limerick.

At much the same time as Constable O'Brien was killed, his colleague Constable Michael Lahiff was walking from Harcourt Street on to St Stephen's Green West. A short time earlier, Commandant Michael Mallin and his ICA battalion had taken over the Green. Constable Lahiff had reached the Unitarian Church when he confronted the ICA and was shot three times. He

died on admission to the Meath Hospital. At the time, and for many years afterwards, Constable Lahiff's death was eclipsed by the controversy about whether or not Countess Markievicz shot him. That controversy lives on, as letters to the *Irish Times* demonstrate. Nevertheless, a 29-year-old, 6ft 4in. unarmed policeman from Killmurray, Co. Clare, was dead. He is buried in Glasnevin Cemetery.

Finally, DMP Constable William Frith was accidentally shot dead at Store Street on the Thursday. Frith, who lived in the Store Street station, had just got out of bed that morning when a bullet came through the window and hit him in the head. It took many questions in the House of Commons by Dublin MP Alfie Byrne and North Cork MP John Healy to establish the source of the bullet. The Royal Irish Rifles were in the area at the time and Sergeant Bannon admitted that he fired shots at the windows. The military said that they were not aware that the building was a police station. Constable Frith was 37. He is buried in Mount Jerome Cemetery.

All seventeen of these men went to work in Easter Week and found themselves in situations not of their making. They paid the ultimate price and have, in the main, been part of a 'hidden history' owing to subsequent events, in particular the War of Independence. But we can assume that these men, like many of their colleagues, were political with a small 'p'. Like 80% of the population, they would have supported the Home Rule policy of John Redmond. In some ways they may even have supported the Sinn Féin policy of 'dual monarchy'.

Whatever their political stance, they left behind devastated families who had to endure the loss of loved ones. The recent inclusion, however, of the names of the fourteen RIC and three DMP policemen killed on duty during the Rising on the memorial erected in Glasnevin Cemetery this year (2016) goes some way towards recognising their passing 100 years ago.

ARMOURED TRUCKS
AND THE RISING

BY **LAR JOYE**

On Easter Monday, 24 April, 1,000 rebels occupied six main positions around Dublin. The response from the British army was to send their mainly Irish regiments to protect Dublin Castle, which was secured within a couple of hours. The remaining buildings were surrounded, and fighting continued until Saturday before the rebels surrendered. Brigadier Lowe, the general in charge, quickly realised that the soldiers needed armoured vehicles, so officers were sent to the Guinness Brewery, where they requisitioned five German-built Daimler three-ton trucks. These were driven just down the road to the workshops of the

Great Southern and Western Railway at Inchicore, where locomotive boilers were attached to the back of three trucks. Loop-holes were cut into the sides to allow for rifle fire, and the cabs were protected by flat steel plates. Two more 'armoured' trucks were created using only flat steel plates, probably because the rail yard had run out of boilers. The speed with which these improvised machines were put together is impressive.

These new armoured vehicles went into action on Wednesday morning. They carried solders from the Royal Irish Regiment from the south quays across Butt Bridge and up to the top of O'Connell Street via

Gardiner Street. Other trucks transported soldiers and equipment to other parts of the north side, in particular around the Four Courts. They were again used by the South Staffordshire Regiment on Friday in the fierce fighting around North King Street, which lasted till Saturday morning. On Saturday 29 April, five Royal Navy Rolls-Royce armoured cars arrived in Dublin, and these were used for patrols over the next few months. The Daimler trucks were returned to Guinness.

●

Below: One of the five German-built Daimler three-ton trucks quickly requisitioned from Guinness Brewery and converted into armoured vehicles. (National Museum of Ireland)

BRITISH ARMY ARTILLERY IN 1916

BY **LAR JOYE**

Artillery dominated the battlefields of the First World War, killing and maiming millions. It could also be used to destroy buildings, to defeat soldiers taking cover within. The British used the eighteen-pounder artillery gun in Dublin in 1916, and the Irish Free State used similar weapons at the beginning of the Civil War in 1922. There were only eight of these in Athlone at the outbreak of the Rising; indeed, only four were in working order, and they were quickly sent to Dublin. Britain's artillery was concentrated in France, of course, in preparation for the Somme offensive that summer.

As in France, however, the eighteen-pounder proved rather ineffective, as it fired a shrapnel shell (like a large grenade) designed to explode above soldiers fighting out in the open. Soldiers in trenches and in buildings could withstand such shelling. What were needed were high-explosive shells. These were developed as the war progressed but were not available in 1916.

A team of seven soldiers, called 'gunners', was required to operate the weapon. An officer received target instructions and calculated the direction and elevation for the gun-layer to point the weapon. Several men set the fuses and delivered shells to the gun, which could fire once every eight seconds. Then it was a matter of firing as fast as possible. In the confines of Dublin City, however, firing would have been at a slower pace.

The four guns were broken into pairs and were used to shell Liberty Hall from just across the river at Tara Street and to destroy barricades on the north side of the city. In the end, most of the destruction in Dublin was due to fires started by both the shelling and the rebels. As it was too dangerous for the Dublin Fire Brigade to tackle the blazes, by Thursday night the city centre was an inferno.

●

Below: The British eighteen-pounder artillery gun used in Dublin in 1916 (and by the Irish Free State at the beginning of the Civil War in 1922). A team of seven gunners was required to operate the weapon, which could fire ten rounds a minute. (National Museum of Ireland)

SPECIFICATIONS

Weight:
1.28 tonnes (1.4 tons)
Calibre:
8.4cm (3.3in.)
Rate of fire:
Ten rounds per minute
Weight of shells:
8.4kg (18.5lb)
Types of shell:
Shrapnel and smoke
Range:
6,000m/6,500 yards
Crew:
Seven
In Irish and British service:
1904–74

THE *HELGA II*

One of the popular myths attached to the Rising is that the city centre was destroyed by shelling from the Royal Navy 'battleship' *Helga*. In truth, the *Helga II* was not a ship of the Royal Navy. She had originally been built in 1908 in Liffey Dockyard for the Department of Agriculture, and she had been pressed into service as an armed yacht during the First World War, serving as an anti-submarine patrol and escort vessel.

When the Rising began, the *Helga* was rushed into position to assist the British army, which lacked enough artillery to fire on the rebel positions. As a result, the *Helga II* gained an undeserved reputation for playing an essential part in Easter Week.

Before the war, the Department of Agriculture and Technical Instruction used the ship for fishery patrols and scientific research,

including a survey of Clare Island from 1909 to 1911. The *Helga* contained a laboratory and it was originally designed as a marine research ship. But in 1915 she was taken over by the admiralty, renamed the HMY *Helga* and classified as an Armed Auxiliary Patrol Yacht. The ship was armed near the bow with a twelve-pounder coastal defence gun, with a range of 11,000 metres. Manned by two sailors, it could fire fifteen rounds a minute. At the rear was a smaller, three-pounder 'pom pom'.

On Tuesday 25 April she sailed from Dún Laoghaire into the Liffey to shell Boland's Mills, and on the following day fired over the loop line railway bridge at Liberty Hall. In total, the *Helga* fired only 40 rounds during the Rising, and it is difficult to assess how effective her guns were. Indeed, two of the ship's crew refused to fire during the engagement.

After 1923 the *Helga* was taken over by the new Irish Department of Agriculture and Fisheries and renamed the *Muirchú* (Seahound). She joined the Marine and Coastwatching Service in 1939. On 8 May 1947, after being retired, she sank off Tuskar Rock *en route* to Dublin to be broken up by the Hammond Lane Foundry Company. In 1951 the Department of Agriculture presented the National Museum with a variety of items associated with the ship, including the *Helga* name-plate, pennants, model and ensign. More recently, the Irish Naval Service has lent the brass ship's bell of the *Muirchú*, which is on display at Collins Barracks.

●

Below: The HMY *Helga*, armed near the bow with a twelve-pounder coastal defence gun. Before the war the ship had been used for fishery patrols and scientific research. She gained an undeserved reputation for playing an essential part in Easter Week.

RIFLES
IN 1916

BY **LAR JOYE**

On 26 July 1914 the *Asgard*, the private yacht of Erskine Childers, then a famous writer, sailed into Howth, north Co. Dublin, carrying 900 Mauser rifles, which were quickly unloaded in 30 minutes and distributed to waiting Irish Volunteers and boys of Fianna Éireann. The landing was a response to the much more successful importation of rifles earlier that year by the Ulster Volunteer Force, which brought in 35,000 German, Italian and Austrian rifles at Larne in April.

The Howth gunrunning, although on a smaller scale, was still heralded as a great success and the rifles were quickly hidden, despite the efforts of the police and the army to intercept the Volunteers. As the shipment was being brought into Dublin city, a British army regiment, the King's Own Scottish Borderers, opened fire on a jeering crowd at Bachelor's Walk: four people were killed and 37 wounded. The next day the remainder of the initial consignment of rifles was landed at Kilcoole, Co. Wicklow. In total, 1,500 rifles were landed, along with 45,000 rounds of ammunition. The landing of the rifles was a public relations coup for the Volunteers.

The Mauser rifle, which quickly became known as the Howth rifle, was designed by Peter Paul Mauser and was the first cartridge rifle adopted by the Prussian army, in 1872. It was a revolutionary design for the 1870s, but by 1914 the German army was using the modern Mauser Gewehr 1898 rifle. Patrick Pearse admitted shortly after the landing that the Mausers were of an 'antiquated pattern, without magazines, and are much inferior to the British service rifle'. Darrell Figgis, who purchased the rifles with The O'Rahilly in Hamburg, described the Mauser as ideal 'for our purpose, cheap and undeniably effective'.

The Mauser *was* an effective weapon, although technically obsolete. It fired a larger bullet than the British Lee Enfield and gave off a lot of smoke when fired, which meant that it was easy to spot Volunteers using the rifle. The other disadvantage was that it could fire only four or five rounds a minute, as it did not have a magazine. British soldiers were trained to fire fifteen rounds a minute with their Lee Enfields, which had ten-round magazines.

One of the legends about the Mauser rifle is that it had a ferocious recoil, as Tom Walsh learned: 'In the excitement I did not heed the lectures and did not hold the gun correctly. The result was that [the first time I fired it] the butt hit me under the chin and knocked me out.' The lack of both training and ammunition meant that many Volunteers had not fired the rifle prior to the Rising.

●

Below: The Lee Enfield 'SMILE Mark III' rifle, standard issue for the British army. It had a ten-round magazine, which allowed the troops to fire fifteen rounds a minute.

●

Bottom: The Prussian Mauser rifle, which became known as the Howth rifle among the Irish Volunteers after its importation. It was technically obsolete but nevertheless proved effective. (Both photographs: National Museum of Ireland)

Lee Enfield SMILE Mark III Rifle

Weight: 3.9kg (8.7lb)
Calibre: 7.7mm (0.303in.)
Magazine: Ten-round magazine
Rate of fire: Fifteen rounds per minute
Range: 2,560m (2,800 yards)
In Irish service: 1922–92

Mauser Model 71 Rifle

Weight: 4.7kg (10.3lb)
Calibre: 11mm (0.43in.)
Magazine: No magazine, single-shot
Rate of fire: Five rounds per minute
Range: 2,930m (3,200 yards)
In Irish service: 1914–23

SIR ROGER CASEMENT AND THE 'IRISH BRIGADE'

BY **LAR JOYE**

During the First World War, Germany considered trying to use Irish resistance to British rule to open another front, both by recruiting captured Irishmen and by providing arms to the Irish Volunteers. In October 1914 Sir Roger Casement, a distinguished British diplomat who had recently taken up the Irish cause, travelled to Berlin. He persuaded Germany to create a new 'Irish Brigade' from among Irish soldiers in the British army captured by Germany. An Irish Brigade raised in eighteenth-century France had become famous fighting for the French against Britain at battles such as Fontenoy in 1745, and Casement hoped to emulate this. In November 1914, 2,486 captive Irish soldiers were separated from their British colleagues and transferred to Limburg.

Irish Volunteer Captain Robert Monteith attempted to recruit soldiers from among these prisoners of war, but the Irish soldiers proved reluctant. There are several explanations for this, not least that the war was still young and its true horrors had not yet become evident. An army brigade normally consists of 3,000 soldiers, but the 'Casement brigade' never numbered more than 60 men. Those who did join were issued a standard German army uniform, adapted to include Irish symbols such as shamrocks and the harp. In the end, the unit never saw action—nor did these 'recruits' receive pensions from the Irish government in the 1920s.

In general, German support for the planned Rising was lukewarm, but they did send a ship, the *Aud*, to bring 20,000 rifles (mostly captured Russian weapons) to the rebels. The Royal Navy captured the ship off the coast of Kerry, however, and she was scuttled by her German crew while being escorted into Cork Harbour.

Soon after, Casement was arrested by the Royal Irish Constabulary on Banna Strand in County Kerry after landing from a U-boat; he was brought to London, tried for treason and hanged in August 1916.

●

Above: A group of the Irish prisoners of war recruited by Irish Volunteer Captain Robert Monteith to join the 'Casement Brigade', which was to help Germany open a new front against Britain. The brigade was never larger than 60 men and never saw action. Members were issued a standard German army uniform, adapted to include Irish symbols such as the shamrock (cap) and the harp (cap and collar). (National Museum of Ireland)

CIVILIANS

HOME FRONT

BY **LUCY McDIARMID**

In the interests of protecting their families, the mothers of the revolutionaries manifested a talent for deception

THE IRISH MAMMY AT THE THRESHOLD OF REBELLION

'As long as you live under my roof you'll do as I say—d'ya hear me?'

'I brought you into this world, and I can take you out just as easy!'

The Irish mammy, as she appears on the internet, asserts her power over house and family in imperious phrases such as those above. In accounts of 1916, too, older women, especially mothers, are responsible for many of the best lines, but few of them left their own records. Áine Heron and Phyllis Morkan, two of the few pregnant women 'out' in Dublin, left witness statements with the Bureau of Military History. But the *bons mots* of an older generation of women, those whose daughters and sons were rebels, appear only as quoted by others.

It's worth looking at the words and deeds of Irish mammies preserved in accounts of the Rising because they show how the mother's authority over the domestic site functioned in a revolutionary context. The Irish home traditionally served as a place where rebellious people and activities were hidden,

●

Left: Nell Humphreys (a sister of The O'Rahilly). On Tuesday Nell went to the GPO, determined to get her twenty-year-old son Dick to come home. She appealed directly to Patrick Pearse, who agreed that Dick should make the sacrifice and leave. (Courtesy of Mark Humphrys, http://humphrysfamilytree.com)

and in 1916 rifles and ammunition were kept under floorboards and inside chimneys. The mammy's authority extended well beyond what could be called the 'domestic', because every inch of the house was potentially a site containing some part of an emergent independent Ireland.

In the interest of protecting their families, then, mothers manifested an admirable talent for deception: it was one form their authority took. Early in 1916, in an apparently spontaneous move, Lillie Connolly adopted a particular maternal role: that of the mother concerned for her daughters' sexual reputation. Two Fianna members from Glasgow arrived at the Connollys' Belfast house with a trunk full of explosives and spent the night there; Ina Connolly arranged for a car to drive them and their luggage to the train station the next morning. While the Connolly daughters were at work, detectives arrived to confront their mother, as Ina tells the story:

'And what is it you are looking for' mother said after they had gone through the house and satisfied themselves there was nobody staying and nothing to trace of visitors having been.

'Well, it's like this. We expected you to have two young men staying here, and you say you did not see anyone staying here. It looks as if you're right.

Now they could not be here without your knowing it. Would you say that's correct?'

'Well, as far as I know, there were no men slept here on Saturday night, for I saw all my family to bed and they were up early in the morning for early Mass and I went down to Crawfordsburn for the day with a friend and returned late at night and went to bed as we have to start early to work on Monday, so I can assure you there was no visitor staying any night here.'

'But, Mrs Connolly, we have information to the effect that two young men came off the Glasgow boat and drove straight here.'

'Well, that might be so,' mother innocently replied, 'without my knowing. You see, I have a couple of girls that the local boys are always after, and when they get my back turned they bring them in and have a ceili in the parlour, dancing and singing to their hearts' content. I never mind. I believe they're safer in the house than running wild on the streets. I thought that some of the neighbours had lodged a complaint and I would not like them to be offensive in any way. Their father would not hear tell of them losing the run of themselves like that.'

The more apologetic she became, the more the detectives tried to calm her down; the more she made a fool of them.

'If you had only told me that on your first visit I could have told you that whatever my girls did they would never keep their boy friends here all night without consulting me, and, of course, I would never put up with that.'

They finally withdrew, satisfied that there was no trace or sign of a visitor or two from Scotland in the vicinity.

This cleverly constructed role played on the expectation that a mother would be guardian of her daughters' virtue. Mrs Connolly also constructed an Irish da with the same concern: he 'would not hear tell of

Left: Mrs Catherine Byrne with her daughters, including Catherine (second from left), who was in the GPO, and Alice (second from right), who was in the ICA. On Easter Monday, when her son Paddy had already 'left for the fight', Mrs Byrne did not scruple to order her daughters out: 'My mother told me to get my equipment and to follow them', wrote Catherine. (The Loane family)

Below left: Kathleen Boland (back left) with Ena Shouldice, and (seated, l–r) Harry Boland, an unknown friend and Jack Shouldice, who fought in North King Street. Kathleen told the Bureau of Military History of her mother's futile attempt to keep Harry out of prison by offering him an alibi. He refused.

Of course, Mrs Daly really *was* a weak old woman, but a clever one who guessed that gender roles might trump politics and that male respect for old mothers might trump British hostility to Irish republicans; she even managed to fool her daughter.

Harry Boland's mother's attempt at deception was not successful, because her son himself rejected it. As his sister Kathleen tells the story in her witness statement for the Bureau of Military History, just after the Rising Mrs Boland went to see her son in Mountjoy before he was sent to prison in England:

> During the course of conversation, my mother who, in her simplicity, thought that she might be able to get Harry out of his difficulty, said, 'Wasn't it an extraordinary thing to arrest you, and you only coming from the races!' But Harry bluntly replied, 'Ah, no, mother. I was not coming from the races. I went out to strike a blow against the bloody British empire'. I can still remember the expression on my mother's face when she realised the hopelessness of her effort to save him.

Even though one of Mrs Boland's ancestors had made pikes for the 1798 rebels, and even though she had said to Harry before the Rising, 'Go, in the name of God! Your father would haunt you if you did not do

them losing the run of themselves like that'.

Mrs Catherine Daly of Limerick, mother of Ned Daly and nine daughters, also deceived from within the domestic site, exploiting her apparent frailty in the national cause. Madge Daly's unpublished memoir (in the Glucksman Library, University of Limerick) tells how a Howth rifle, ceremonially given to her uncle, the Fenian John Daly, was saved during a raid on the Dalys' house:

> We had the Howth rifle which was presented to my uncle after the gunrunning [inscribed by many of the men who later became signatories of the 'Proclamation'] and two miniature rifles and some revolvers. The guns were rolled up in a large carpet, which lay against the wall. My mother sat in a large armchair in front of the roll. She was very frail and delicate-looking and managed to get a weakness but when my sister went over to help her she gave a wink. My sister nearly roared laughing … The soldiers were very sympathetic and did not like to disturb her, so her wit saved the guns. The padded armchairs were packed with ammunition, but it was not discovered.

the right thing', she nevertheless attempted a maternal lie to keep her son out of prison.

Almost every one of the rebels had a mammy behind him or her—not always, like Mrs Boland, trying to save him from prison, but more often protecting him within the domestic site with the traditional maternal forms of nurturing. When, at the surrender, Con Colbert was standing in place outside the Marrowbone Lane distillery, in his pocket (wrote Annie Cooney O'Brien) were 'a piece of my mother's brown bread' and a sock that Annie had darned. In Wexford, as the Rising in Dublin was beginning, John Furlong's mother said to the Volunteers in her house, 'So you are going out. Thanks be to God I lived to see this day', and gave them dry socks and 'a hearty breakfast'.

For the four days before the Rising, the O'Kelly family played host to Patrick and Willie Pearse, whose school the O'Kelly brothers attended. According to the witness statement of their sister, Mairéad Ní Cheallaigh, the drawing-room was given over to the Pearses, and their weapons and ammunition were hidden there: 'I did not see the revolvers which must have been in the haversacks which were buckled up and were never opened in my presence. Pádraig asked my mother would their stuff be safe there. My mother reassured them, saying no one would enter the room without their permission.' Mrs O'Kelly also purchased 'nice linen' towels for 'these important and distinguished guests'.

In a memorable passage, Ní Cheallaigh described serving the Pearse brothers what must have been their last home-cooked meal:

'My mother ... called me to give me instructions about the breakfast for the Pearses. She said she had prepared a tureen of bacon and eggs, which she had left on a trivet in front of the dining-room fire. She had also a tureen of mutton chops. She said they must be very hungry and God knows when they will get a meal again. She must have known more than

I did. She went out and I went into the dining-room where the table was set. Shortly afterwards I heard the Pearses come down stairs. They stood shyly outside the door until I called them in. I informed them that my mother had been worried about their taking so little food and had prepared their breakfast herself. I said I hoped they would enjoy it. I placed the two tureens on the table and they ate every bit of the food on the table, including a whole loaf of bread.

The men about to begin an armed revolution were too shy or too polite to enter the dining-room uninvited. The rooms in the household were gendered in different ways: the drawing-room where the brothers stashed their guns and ammunition was off limits to everyone else, but the dining-room was under the control of the women, with the mammy's authority dominant; it was she who cooked the food, filled the tureens and gave the order that the men must eat. Ní Cheallaigh was 'dumbfounded', she adds, 'to see all they had eaten'.

The mother's control over the domestic site, expressed in the willingness to deceive and the authority to feed, extended also to the boundaries defined by architectural features. This control included both the power to go beyond boundaries and the power to maintain them. On the Tuesday of Easter Week, Robert Brennan's mother (in Wexford) learned that he was not out because of the countermanding order, and he could not himself give an order because, as he said, 'I have no authority'. Mrs Brennan had no trouble giving orders or finding a source of authority: 'Go up there to the room,' she said, 'and kneel down in front of the Sacred Heart and you'll get your authority.' On the Monday of Easter Week, when Paddy Byrne of Dublin and other men had already 'left for the fight', Mrs Byrne did not scruple to order her daughters out: 'My mother told me to get my equipment and to follow them', wrote Catherine Byrne Rooney. By

the time the official mobilising order came from Cumann na mBan, Catherine was already in the GPO and her sister Alice with the Citizen Army.

The mother's authority to keep her children within the house provoked discussion by rebel leaders in the GPO on at least two occasions. When Seán McLoughlin saw his fifteen-year-old sister Mary in the Post Office, he was not encouraging. As Mary McLoughlin wrote in her witness statement, 'Seán told me to go home to my mother, that she was looking everywhere for me and would kill me when she saw me. Seán MacDermott, who was standing by, said "Your mother won't kill you. She will live to be proud of you".' When young Mary went home to check on her mother, the little drama that ensued was not what MacDermott had imagined:

... mother opened the door and what a surprise she got when she saw me. 'Well my fine rossie, but I'm glad to see you and to have you home again and I intend to keep you safe with me', said she ... She brought me upstairs, put me into a room and locked me in,

●

Below: Mary McLoughlin, pictured on the right with Hanna Sheehy Skeffington and Kathleen Lynn (centre), was locked in her room by her mother to prevent her return to the GPO—'an extreme assertion of the mammy's power'. This ploy did not work. (© Christina McLoughlin)

saying, 'You will be safer there for a few days. I will go and get you some food. You must be starving, my poor child'. With that she departed before I got the chance of saying one word. Realising I was locked in a room and that I was in possession of a gun, I turned towards the window and there I saw my opportunity of clearing out and bringing the gun back again to the GPO. It did not take me long to get out of the window …

Locking a child in a room is an extreme assertion of the mammy's power. Although Mrs McLoughlin was not able to maintain the domestic boundary, she is at least on record as uttering the wonderful Irish slang word 'rossie' (brat).

The O'Rahilly's sister, Nell Humphreys, was just as determined to get her child home and out of the GPO. Dick was twenty years old, but Mrs Humphreys (who had earlier tried 'to persuade Pearse to give up his protest and leave the GPO', as her daughter Sighle wrote) sallied forth on Tuesday to 'concentrate on bringing Dick home'.

When she explained to Pearse how if anything happened to Michael and Dick, the two families would be left with no man, Pearse readily saw her point and advised Dick to accompany her home. He very kindly added that he had shown/proved [sic] himself willing to fight and die for Ireland, but that he should now make the sacrifice of going home to help both his families. Being thus ordered by Pearse to go home, he said good bye to his Commander in General and to Michael, to whom he whispered, 'I'll be back'.

Dick and his mother were shot at on the way home and, he noted, 'he was much safer in the PO'. After Mass and breakfast next morning, Dick 'announced that he was returning to the GPO. This time my mother did not try to stop him.'

As a figure asserting power over a politicised domestic site, the Irish mammy features prominently in many accounts of the Rising. She is not a Kathleen Ní Houlihan; her realm is the practical, not the allegorical. She doesn't always send her children to a martyr's death: sometimes she locks them in the house or tries to get them home from battle. She cooks mutton chops and offers clean socks. She invokes the Sacred Heart for help with military decisions. The 1916 mammies, as they are represented by others, do not have a single, consistent political position, but they all hover over the house's threshold, dominant and quotable.

Lucy McDiarmid's most recent book is At home in the revolution: what women said and did in 1916 *(Royal Irish Academy).*

Further reading

Robert Brennan, *Allegiance* (Dublin, 1950).
Bureau of Military History: witness statements by Ina Connolly Heron, Mary McLoughlin, Mairéad Ní Cheallaigh, Annie (Cooney) O'Brien, Kathleen (Boland) O'Donovan, Catherine (Byrne) Rooney (http://www.bureauofmilitaryhistory.ie/).
Lucy McDiarmid, *At home in the revolution: what women said and did in 1916* (Dublin, 2015).
Madge Daly, 'The Memoirs of Madge Daly' (typescript, Glucksman Library, University of Limerick).

Left: Mrs Catherine Daly of Limerick, mother of Ned, with five of her nine daughters. Her daughter Madge recalled how her frail-looking mother had feigned a weakness to distract soldiers who were searching the house for weapons. (© Mairéad and Nora de hÓir. Courtesy of Kilmainham Gaol Museum, 17PC-I B52-05)

LOOTING

BY **PADRAIG YEATES**

Image: These young women look delighted with their haul of potential firewood collected from the ruins of buildings. (National Museum of Ireland)

Despite the risk of being shot, struck by shrapnel, crushed by falling buildings or burnt to death, looters remained dedicated to their task

LOOTERS, DESERTERS AND 'ORDINARY DECENT CRIMINALS' IN 1916

The mobs that looted Dublin's city centre in 1916 have entered the mythology of the Rising just as robustly as the Irish Volunteers and the Irish Citizen Army.

The military commander of the revolutionaries, James Connolly, initially dismissed the looters as 'one more problem for the British',[1] but he soon sent out members of the GPO garrison to disperse them by firing over their heads. It had little effect. Nearby, Liam Archer, an Irish Volunteer section commander in the Church Street area, recalled on the first evening of the Rising the 'holidaymakers on their way home, and looters, [who] sought to pass through [the barricades]. The former we passed through in convoyed groups; the latter we stripped of all their loot and tried to frighten with dire threats.'[2] Members of the Citizen Army seem to have taken a harsher view of the looters than Irish Volunteers, perhaps because their behaviour reflected so badly on the honour of a working class which they sought to elevate to higher things.

Despite the not inconsiderable risk of being shot, struck by shrapnel, crushed by falling buildings or burnt to death as they went about unlawful business, looters remained dedicated to their task as long as there was loot to be had. We must assume that they comprised a significant number of the civilian casualties in Easter Week.

We can at last identify some of the looters and those who benefited from the proceeds thanks to the rediscovery of the DMP (Dublin Metropolitan Police) Prisoners Book for 1916–1918. This lists everyone 'Charged with Offences involving dishonesty'. As a result, we can learn a great deal about those involved in looting and in crime in general in 1916 Dublin.

Normally, male offenders far exceeded women. In January women comprised only 19% of those arrested, in February 17%, in March 16% and in April 18%. But in May the number of women arrested rose to 57%, and in June it was still 27%. They also accounted for 80% of those arrested for illegal possession in the police raids that followed the Rising. In May, married women (including widows) overtook British army deserters and juveniles as the largest group of offenders in the city. The widows involved would, after two years of war, presumably include a significant number of war widows. Unfortunately, in the vast majority of cases no description is given of the goods repossessed by the DMP, but only four cases of illegal possession of porter are recorded, as compared with seventeen of flour, twelve of household items such as chinaware, nine of bicycles, six of boots, two of sugar, two of footballs and one each of soap and a perambulator. These seizures suggest women who were using a rare opportunity to stock up on essential items for their families rather than the dissolute, drink-crazed harpies beloved by nationalist propagandists. At the same time, there are far too many descriptions of inebriates of both sexes to doubt their existence. Presumably many would have been too drunk to loot much other than 'ardent spirits'.

Police magistrates generally imposed fines of anything from 5s. to 40s. on looters, presumably reflecting the value of the items found, and quite a lot of women with children appear to have been let off with a caution. The magistrates also tended to inflict harsher sentences on male offenders. A labourer caught with a 'Cartload of Loot' was given a month's imprisonment, while a married woman arrested in the same general location with another 'Cartload of Loot' was fined 20s. Altogether 49 women out of 443 charged with illegal possession received prison sentences (11%), compared with 35 out of 179 men (19.5%). Three men were sentenced to six months and a seventeen-year-old labourer to three years in Borstal, while the heaviest sentence given to a woman was two months with hard labour. Recipients of the latter sentence included a prostitute and a lady housekeeper. The heavier sentences for men sometimes reflected aggravating factors such as larceny and warehouse- or shop-breaking, rather than the relatively passive charges of illegal possession or receiving.

There was quite a diversity of social backgrounds. Married women accounted for 44% and widows for 7% of looters, or just over half of the total. Looters with no occupation are the next largest group at 14%. Two thirds of them were also women, many of no fixed abode. Two predictable groups among the prisoners are the nineteen dealers and 58 labourers. All but two of the dealers are women, reflecting their dominance in this occupation. The number of labourers is surprisingly small, given that they constituted almost a quarter of the adult male population. By comparison, messengers are over-represented, reflecting the high level of juvenile crime.

Porters are another over-represented group and not one popularly associated with the 1916 looting phenomenon.

By contrast, few prostitutes were charged. Nor does the presence of skilled workers such as bricklayers, a boiler-maker, engineer (fitter), printer, bookbinder and two cabinet-makers conform with the traditional image of the looter. The presence of a moneylender, a publican and a licensed general dealer may be an indication of a network for feloniously receiving and recycling stolen goods. The records tell us only that the publican was fined £3 for receiving; the case against the moneylender was discharged and the fate of the licensed general dealer is not recorded. It is possible that they traded information for leniency.

The great unsolved crime of the Rising is the theft of £5,000 worth of merchandise from the British and Irish Steam Packet Company warehouse on the North Wall. The only people with the organisation, freedom of movement and local knowledge capable of carrying out such an operation were probably Dubliners in the British army. The culprits are unlikely ever to be identified.

DESERTERS, ABSENTEES AND JUVENILE DELINQUENTS

If the looting phenomenon can be related to the Rising, a more serious problem in 1916 was desertion and absenteeism from the armed forces.[3] These two groups accounted for

NMI Collection

• Above: Archibald McGoogan's chromolithographic print *After the bombardment. The holocaust of Ireland's greatest thoroughfare, Friday Morning, 29th April, 1916.* McGoogan was the first photographer employed by the National Museum of Ireland. (NLI)

• Left: A photo/map referencing some of the immediate popular response to the events of Easter Monday. It is likely that looters comprised a significant number of the civilian casualties. (NMI Collection)

●
Left: The Cable Shoe Co. and the Munster and Leinster Bank. The Cable Shoe Co. was emptied of goods—it was reported that looters returned if the first pair didn't fit properly. Both buildings were gutted by the fires. (NLI)

●
Below left: A contemporary view of the façade of the B&I Steam Packet Company premises. Merchandise worth £5,000 was appropriated from the company's warehouse on the North Wall.

Desertion and absenteeism were major problems for all belligerents during the war, particularly in multinational states or places such as Ireland where identification with the metropolitan power was relatively weak. Deserters in Dublin included fugitives from Britain and from the BEF in France. Some of these men were certainly British and may have been under the illusion that the absence of conscription in Ireland somehow protected them. Only one deserter was arrested while begging during the first half of 1916, and another was found sleeping rough. Clearly the majority of soldiers on the run were sheltered by relatives and friends, in spite of the penalties for harbouring deserters. That January, a nineteen-year-old weaver in Meath Street was given six weeks' hard labour for doing so, presumably for a relation or boyfriend. A soldier's wife and female accomplice were fined 10s. each in March for obstructing his arrest. In April a 59-year-old postman and his wife were arrested for harbouring their son and assisting his escape.

Many deserters were caught after committing other offences, such as malicious damage, assault or being drunk and disorderly. The prevalence of this type of antisocial behaviour among soldiers far exceeds such cases before 1914 and may reflect psychological and emotional problems derived from wartime service. Normally men were handed straight over to the military authorities. Very occasionally they received prison sentences, which, perversely, provided an incentive to serious

44% of all men arrested in January 1916, no doubt with Christmas leave contributing significantly to the numbers. They comprised 37% of arrests in February, 27% in March and 37% in April. In May the number dropped to 16%, possibly because the Rising may have skewed figures. They rose again to 23% in June, 30% in July, 38% in August, 34% in both September and October, 19% in November and 42% in December.

crime if a soldier's main reason for not returning to his unit was to avoid being sent to the front. Only a handful of sailors appear to have jumped ship in Dublin, possibly because it had no naval base.

After desertion and absenteeism, juvenile crime was the largest problem confronting the DMP. Juveniles actually overtook soldiers as the largest group of offenders in May and June. Offences ranged from stealing sweets to housebreaking. In fact, housebreaking by teenage gangs exceeded such activities by adults; whether their activities were organised by adults is unclear, but often women charged with receiving stolen goods lived in the same locations as the juveniles arrested. The other major activity of juvenile gangs was larceny of coal and other imported goods. Prices had soared as U-boat activity pushed up the cost of shipping.

The war led to a proliferation of military property, which was considered fair game not only by professional criminals but also by militant nationalists and soldiers anxious to supplement their pitiful wages of a shilling a day.[4] Arrests for feloniously receiving items such as khaki shirts and handkerchiefs, military blankets, boots or buckles—and even in one case an army donkey—are recorded.

A new area of white-collar crime for women was defrauding the War Office with false claims for separation payments. Fraudulent enlistment, always prevalent in Dublin, increased after the outbreak of war. Penalties for offenders were severe. A married woman received three months' hard labour in January for defrauding the War Office, and a man convicted of fraudulent enlistment in February was sentenced to two months' hard labour. Even minor offences such as the theft of a pair of army drawers attracted the options of a month in prison or a 40s. fine, as well as £10 bail.

The treatment of militant nationalists was often less severe than that dealt out to people seeking to rob or defraud the War Office. Only one man was brought before the police magistrates before the

Easter Rising for a breach of the Defence of the Realm Act.

Firearms offences were treated leniently, given that Britain was engaged in a life-or-death struggle with Imperial Germany. In January 1916 a 40-year-old widow was fined £2 for unlawful possession of a service rifle. Only six men were convicted of offences relating to possession of service rifles between January and the Rising, with sentences varying from two to six months— this in a city bristling with guns. A regime that devoted more resources to dealing with fraudulent claims for separation allowances than to disarming private militias was certainly suffering from a lethal form of political myopia.

As in peacetime, very few middle-class people were charged with any offence, and even more rarely convicted. When John Lemass, a sixteen-year-old student living in Capel Street, was charged with manslaughter after a gun killed his baby brother Herbert in January, the case went nowhere because information was refused. No convictions were secured in two other fatal shooting incidents that month, one involving an auctioneer and the other a grocer's assistant. There were no arrests by

the DMP for firearms offences in May or June.

Sexually related crimes reported in Dublin in the first half of 1916 were also rare. The handful of people charged were mainly outsiders, including members of the British army.

To read the DMP log you would never guess that revolution was fomenting in Dublin, but you would know that there was a war going on.

NOTES
1. BMHWS 1766 William O'Brien.
2. BMHWS 819 Liam Archer.
3. A man absent from his unit for more than 30 days was deemed a deserter.
4. Soldiers were entitled to extra allowances for extra competencies so that average pay was about 1s. 9d, but the average for infantrymen was probably lower, as opportunities to acquire extra skills were limited.

●

Below: A later picture of 'Monto', an area of Dublin noted for brothel-keeping. According to DMP records, married women accounted for 44% and widows for 7% of looters, or just over half of the total. By contrast, few prostitutes were charged. (Courtesy of Terry Fagan, North Inner City Folklore Project)

Many children were shot in crossfire as they scavenged, played, ran and revelled in the mayhem

INNOCENTS LOST AND FORGOTTEN

'Seven children were killed in the area around the fruit market alone, making the Church Street environs the bloodiest spot for children during Easter Week'

'Small boys bolted in to see these sights and bolted out again with bullets quickening their feet. Small boys do not believe that people will really kill them, but small boys were killed.'[1]

The most dangerous place in the world for children during Easter 1916 was the centre of Dublin: 40 young people aged sixteen and under died violently in the Rising. Two still remain unidentified; there are death certificates stating clearly that they died of gunshot wounds between 24 and 30 April, but we know little else. There are, according to the National Museum, up to 30 unidentified civilians.[2] That this should be the case 100 years after

●

Left: Members of the Catholic Boys' Brigade, Church Street. (Irish Capuchin Archives)

the insurrection is beyond belief.

During the six-day rebellion, 77 rebels, over 120 British uniformed forces and over 300 civilians were killed. Clearly, the vast majority of victims were non-combatants. In one sense this is not surprising; after all, well over 20,000 armed combatants had fought it out within a compact, concentrated urban space teeming with people. In the words of one rebel, 'it was pouring bullets'.

Any child shot in the head— and there were thirteen of them— died instantly. Other children, most of whom were shot in the stomach, had little chance of survival, given the type of bullets used and the surgical knowledge and medicines available at the time, combined with the difficulty doctors had in reaching the city-centre hospitals.

Obviously, those children who would otherwise have been in school were off for the Easter holidays, but

twelve of the children who died were already working. The allure, light and excitement of street life, as opposed to the cramped, dark, dank conditions of the city tenements, meant that many children were shot in crossfire as they scavenged, played, ran and revelled in the mayhem, commotion and excitement in that magnificent late April sunlight.

Children in the Dublin of 100 years ago had the run of the city centre. As one observer put it, 'in no city in these islands with which I am acquainted have the children such freedom, I might say such possession of the streets as Dublin'.[3] But the excitement of the Rising also had a fatal attraction. As the word flew

●
Left: The story of the first child killed during the Rising neatly reflects the complicated network of allegiances which prevailed in the Dublin of the time. Early on Monday afternoon Seán Francis Foster, just shy of his third birthday, was shot in the head by a stray bullet as his mother Katie wheeled him and his infant brother in their pram down Church Street, near the Four Courts. Katie was on her way to attend the Feis Maitiú, that celebration of native Irish culture. She was already a widow. Her husband, John, Seán's father, had been a cooper at Guinness' and a member of the British army reserve. After being called up, he was declared missing in action in

early May 1915 while serving with the Royal Irish Rifles on the Western Front. On her way to the feis, Katie had discovered her brother, Joseph O'Neill, among a group of Irish Volunteers manning a barricade at the corner of Church Street and North King Street. Just then, a party of mounted British army lancers rode into view and the Volunteers opened fire. Katie and Seán (left, pictured in a locket) were caught in the crossfire. While it was never clear which side had fired the fatal shot, Katie never doubted that it had come from the revolver of one of her brother's colleagues. (Courtesy of the Foster family and Hachette Books Ireland)

around the city centre from noon on Monday, children swarmed into the centre—often with their parents—to see what the commotion was about. The sense of giddiness and expectation that had permeated the city for the few months beforehand had suddenly exploded into an almost spontaneous conflagration.

The rebels gazing out the broken windows of the GPO—rifles at the ready, awaiting the British onslaught—looked on in horror as civilians promenaded by on a sunny bank holiday, and watched aghast as a few broke ranks and grabbed whatever free stuff was available. As the unsold Easter eggs in Noblett's window were snatched by children who had never before tasted chocolate, the looting began. Most of the looting took place in and around Sackville Street and was in full flow by Monday evening. Nowhere was safe: grocers, butchers, pubs, clothing and shoe shops were hit with abandon, the looters driven by opportunity, hunger, need and sheer wonderment. Push, shove, grab, elbow, run, escape!

The rebels, however, took a much dimmer view of their rampaging fellow city-dwellers. Seán T. O'Kelly—a future president of Ireland—was sent out from the GPO to stop the looters, but he was powerless. On his return, Commandant James Connolly admonished him: 'Shooting over their heads is useless. Unless a few of them are shot you won't stop them. I'll have to send someone over there who'll deal with the looters.'[4] There is no evidence, by the way, that Connolly's command was carried out; the story is more an indication of the desperation the rebels may have felt as they looked at the mayhem: is this what we are sacrificing our lives for?

To get a glimpse of the chaos that enveloped the centre of Dublin one has only to look at the date, location and ages of the children killed that fateful week. All of them were killed within a very small part of Dublin, an area defined by the Royal Canal on the north side and the Grand Canal on the south side, effectively within a 2km radius of the GPO. And most died close to their homes. No child deaths are recorded west of Kingsbridge (Heuston) Station or east of the Customs House. Four areas account for the majority of child deaths: Sackville Street (12), Church Street (8), around the Jacob's biscuit factory (7) and St Stephen's Green (7).

In the vast majority of cases we are unable to find out who shot them. Yes, Christopher Hickey was killed by British soldiers in the North King Street massacre, while Bridget McKane was accidentally shot by rebels in the retreat from the GPO on Friday night. There were no inquests, however, so for the most part we simply can't be certain who shot them.

Given the age of the children and the chaos and confusion of the week, it is not surprising that the details are sketchy. And, obviously, none had direct descendants. But their violent ends are verified by death certificates, family stories, burial records and compensation claims. The lack of detail also goes some way towards explaining why they were simply forgotten for nearly 100 years. And by the time interest had been shown in this aspect of the

●

Below: A photograph from the *Daily Mirror* of 5 May 1916, showing Volunteers under arrest being escorted by British soldiers. There are at least one or maybe two youngsters involved, and perhaps one child observing. (Irish Capuchin Archives)

Rising, many of those who had any connection with or memory of these young children were themselves gone.

Of the 38 identified children, I have managed to contact relatives of 26. Each family believes that the names of the children should be commemorated publicly in the city, for not only were they the unknown dead of Easter Week but the majority were buried in unmarked graves.

By the end of the first day of the Rising nine children had been killed. The first child casualty on Easter Monday was two-year-old Seán Frances Foster, hit in his pram by a stray bullet in Church Street. The story of baby Foster encapsulates the complexity of the Rising. His father, an employee of Guinness, had been killed the previous year fighting in France. His uncle, Joseph O'Neill, was outside on the barricades with the Irish Volunteers, taking on the might of the British, and his mother had been heading to help with the Feis Maitiú when she got caught in the crossfire that killed her second-eldest child.

Across the river, in the vicinity of Jacob's biscuit factory in Bishop Street, three children were killed. Near the GPO, Patrick Fetherston (12)

was shot near the top of O'Connell (Sackville) Street as he scooted around in a makeshift boxcar—with perhaps some innocent looting involved. By the time his mother had wheeled him to Jervis Street hospital in his boxcar he had bled to death. In the space of 60 minutes Paddy's homemade transport was his vehicle to adventure, his ambulance and his hearse. Another child, John Kirwan (12), was last seen playing outside Elvery's sports shop that afternoon. It took a full month, and a plea from his mother, for his body to be found in Jervis Street hospital; he was identified by a 'lucky sixpence' that he had carried since his confirmation.

Tuesday, Wednesday and Thursday saw thirteen children killed, while Friday was again catastrophic. Food shortages and starvation threatened and the city became a bloodbath for children, with many scavenging for food: at least eleven died. Two children were killed behind the GPO as the rebels retreated.

Seven children died after the surrender on Saturday 29 April. The last child to die as a direct result of the Rising was eight-year-old Walter Scott; he had been wounded during the week, then developed septi-

caemia and died on 5 July.

If you divide the centre of Dublin into four quadrants—with the Liffey as the north–south line, and the east–west line running from O'Connell Street though Grafton Street to the canal—you get a fairly equal death rate. The bloodiest area of the city was west of the GPO, with thirteen dead. Seven children were killed in the area around the fruit market alone, making the Church Street environs the bloodiest spot for children during Easter Week. Six were killed near the Jacob's factory in Bishop Street. Mount Street Bridge was another black spot, with three children dying violently.

Thirty-one boys and nine girls were killed, either from 'gunshot wounds' or 'cannonading'. Thirty-five were Roman Catholic and five were Protestant. Twenty-three lived in the horrific tenement conditions, others were in 'artisans' dwellings'. Five could be fairly described as

●
Above: Children in Gardiner Street Convent School in 1923. Their bare feet and evident poverty would have been typical of children in 1916. But these children seem in good health, perhaps a testament to the food they receive at the school. (Irish Capuchin Archives)

It was a frenetic week, a cauldron between the canals. Children, many from the tenements, captured the streets, careering recklessly; others were simply out playing in the sunshine. Forty young lives cut short, most buried in unmarked graves. But there remains something innocent and childlike in their lives that gloriously sunny week.

What was the taste in their young mouths as they died amid the battle for Irish freedom? One hundred years later, we can only hope that they did taste the sweetness of youth and the excitement of a changing world before they were caught in the crossfire, becoming the children of our revolution.

'Possibly most of the looters are children who are having the sole gorge of their lives. They have tasted sweet stuff they had never toothed before, and will never taste again in this life, and until they die the insurrection of 1916 will have a sweet savour for them.'[5]

Further reading

Joe Duffy, *Children of the Rising: the untold story of the young lives lost during Easter 1916* (Hachette Ireland, 2015).

NOTES

1. James Stephens, *The insurrection in Dublin* (London, 1916), chapter 3.
2. Brenda Malone, Senior Researcher, National Library of Ireland.
3. John Cooke, Honorary Treasurer of the National Society for the Prevention of Cruelty to Children, at the Dublin Housing Inquiry, 1913.
4. Seán T. O'Kelly, 'Easter Week experiences', *Irish Press*, 6–9 August 1961.
5. Stephens, *The insurrection in Dublin*, chapter 2.

●

Above left: A young street newspaper vendor posing in a studio, also a member of the Catholic Boys' Brigade, Church Street. His bare feet and poor clothing were clearly not a barrier to a broad smile. Hopefully, he was one who did live to experience 'the sweetness of youth and the excitement of a changing world'. (Irish Capuchin Archives)

coming from well-off backgrounds.

Four of the children were in uniform when they were killed. Charles Darcy (16) was a member of the Irish Citizen Army and was killed beside Dublin Castle, while Seán Healy (14) and James Fox (15) were members of Na Fianna. All were no more than messenger boys, but they were 'out' in 1916 against the wishes of either their parents or their commanders—or both. Neville

Fryday, originally from Tipperary, was in a Canadian Army uniform and was on Easter leave, visiting his mother in Glasnevin before he was due to be sent to the Somme. He was recorded as being absent without leave on Tuesday 25 April. In fact, he had been shot by a sniper as he walked past Trinity College early on Easter Monday afternoon. His two soldier brothers who had preceded him to the Western Front survived the war.

REFLECTION
INTERNATIONAL BY MAURICE WALSH
CONTEXT

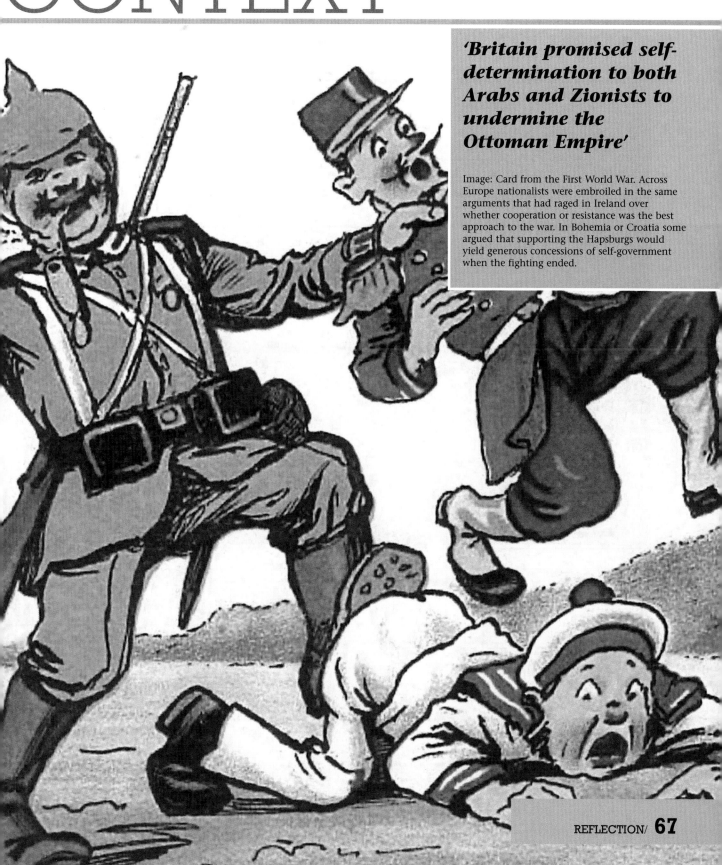

'Britain promised self-determination to both Arabs and Zionists to undermine the Ottoman Empire'

Image: Card from the First World War. Across Europe nationalists were embroiled in the same arguments that had raged in Ireland over whether cooperation or resistance was the best approach to the war. In Bohemia or Croatia some argued that supporting the Hapsburgs would yield generous concessions of self-government when the fighting ended.

The war had delivered to new and smaller nations an unrivalled chance to strike a blow for freedom

EMPIRE'S DIFFICULTY WAS EVERYBODY'S OPPORTUNITY

I n 1916 John Buchan published *Greenmantle*, his second novel featuring the intrepid British agent Richard Hannay. Replicating the instant success of *The thirty-nine steps*, published the previous year, the story of the attempt to thwart a German-inspired Muslim uprising in the Middle East sold more than 30,000 copies within months (Ernie O'Malley became a confirmed Buchan fan when he read the book while a republican prisoner in Mountjoy).

The success of the novels owed much to the fact that Buchan was already making a name for himself as a chronicler of the unfolding Great War, a mixture of contemporary historian, journalist and propagandist. The first volume of his *Nelson's history of the war* had appeared in February 1915, seven months before *The thirty-nine steps*, and the series would even-

tually run to 24 volumes, over a million words. In 1922, compressed to four volumes but largely unaltered, it was republished as *A history of the Great War*, the first extensive survey of the vast conflagration that had reshaped the world.

Buchan devoted a few pages to the Easter Rising; his verdict was dismissive. 'This tragic episode had small bearing on the war', he wrote; it merely demonstrated that Ireland 'had dropped out of the brotherhood of nations' and had shown itself to be 'at variance, not with Britain but with civilisation'.

It is easy to see how, to a fervently patriotic Englishman, the week-long uprising in Dublin would seem insignificant in the context of the colossal slaughter at the Somme and the ferocious battles in Mesopotamia. Fifty years later Conor Cruise O'Brien argued (in hindsight, obviously) that if the insurrectionists had waited until 1918, when most of the country was united against conscription and Britain and its allies were on the back foot, the Rising could have changed the course of world history. But it is not necessary to adhere to either of these extremes to see the Rising as a significant international event.

By 1916 the war between the major powers that had once been predicted to end by Christmas 1914 had unexpectedly developed into a complicated worldwide conflagration. Despite the British blockade of Germany, mass sacrifice on the Western Front—the French lost one and a half million men in that year—and the disastrous Gallipoli campaign, the obduracy of the Central Powers had failed to break. The war was also being industrialised. Generals from all armies bemoaned the lack of munitions, and factories and civilians were enlisted to produce armaments. In Britain, volunteer enthusiasm

● Above left: John Buchan, a fervently patriotic Englishman, devoted just a few pages to the Rising in his *A history of the Great War*; his verdict was dismissive. It merely demonstrated that Ireland 'had dropped out of the brotherhood of nations' and had shown itself to be 'at variance, not with Britain but with civilisation'.

could no longer be counted on to replace casualties; conscription was introduced in imitation of the mass armies of the Continent.

The threat of the extension of compulsory enlistment to Ireland gripped the popular imagination. For radical nationalists, for whom the war was an opportunity for a running commentary debunking recruitment propaganda, this potentially sinister

turn was a gift. Instead of ridiculing those who joined the allied armies, separatists now portrayed them as victims, brave men betrayed by the incompetence of British generals. The extensive Irish casualties at Suvla Bay in the summer of 1915 had epitomised the callous wastage of lives and found new resonance with popular feeling.

The changing attitude towards the war was a sign of how its extraordinary scope and scale made it much more disruptive than anyone could have foreseen. At the start, empires had been mobilised as if they were ancient nations. But suddenly the war delivered to new and smaller nations an unrivalled opportunity to mobilise against empire; empire's difficulty was everybody's opportunity. Across Europe, nationalists were embroiled in the same arguments that had raged in Ireland over whether cooperation or resistance was the best approach to the war. In Bohemia or Croatia some argued that supporting the Hapsburgs would yield generous concessions of self-government when the fighting ended. But more radical nationalists believed that the war presented a chance to strike a blow for freedom, and they formed secret committees to plot revolt.

This ferment of nationalism was not driven solely by inspired opportunism. It is now a commonplace that Patrick Pearse's rhetoric celebrating youthful aggression and bloody sacrifice as the saviours of national values from the deadening modernity enveloping the world was echoed all over Europe. But other ideas had also gained a wide following. Well before Woodrow Wilson arrived to promulgate self-determination, British liberal thinkers and statesmen were championing the 'nationality principle', not just in defence of Belgium from German invasion but as a solution to the problems that had caused the war. 'There can be no good international system,' Bertrand Russell wrote, 'until the boundaries of states coincide as nearly as possible with the boundaries of nations.'

For the main belligerents, backing nationalism was also a tempting tactic for less idealistic reasons. Stir-

ring up discontent among the peoples of the enemy empires was another way of prosecuting the war. Britain promised self-determination to both Arabs and Zionists to undermine the Ottoman Empire, and sponsored the Congress of Oppressed Nationalities to bring together Poles, Czechs, Croats and Slovenes keen to liberate themselves from Austria-Hungary. Germany called for a jihad of Muslims in the British, French and Russian empires (showing that Buchan's fiction was not mere fantasy). Finnish, Georgian, Persian and Indian revolutionaries were welcomed in Berlin alongside Roger Casement. 'German declarations for the Irish, the Poles, the Jews, the Finns etc. could only have a positive effect here,' the Kaiser's ambassador in the US cabled home. The Germans provided arms to the Mexican revolutionary Pancho Villa and promised that a future alliance would result in the recovery of Texas, Arizona and New Mexico.

This held an element of plausibility, since Germany had all the appearances of an emerging world power, tailgating Britain in the race for global dominance. By the eve of the war the German navy was challenging the Royal Navy, and the country was threatening to surpass Britain as the world's leading exporter, with its scientists and engineers making companies such as Siemens and AEG trail-blazers in design and innovation in the most modern industries based on electricity. Wilhelm II hailed the arrival of the 'German century'. Casement was convinced that the days of Britain's supremacy were numbered; Arthur Griffith held Germany to be 'a paragon of morals, cultural values and learning'; and James Connolly contrasted Germany's very civilised people with the 'many millions of barbarians' under Russian rule. 'To help Britain is to help Russia to the dominance of Europe,' he wrote right at the beginning of the war, 'to help the barbarian to crush the scientist.'

Casement idealised Germany as the liberator of small nations, believing that Berlin could be persuaded to send thousands of its soldiers to sup-

Above: Pancho Villa: the Germans provided arms to the Mexican revolutionary and promised that a future alliance would result in the recovery of Texas, Arizona and New Mexico.

port an insurrection in Ireland. Nationalist propaganda insisted that German invaders would treat the Irish well. As with the British, however, the national aspirations of other peoples were subordinate to German imperial interests. Far from being the benign liberator that Casement imagined, Germany planned to consolidate an empire across the continent, occupying territory to the east and west to protect the motherland from invasion, a *Mitteleuropa* that would be run according to a strict racial hierarchy in which non-Germans would be treated as disenfranchised natives of a vast colony.

Belatedly, Casement realised that the Irish, just like the Mexicans, the Finns and the rest, were pawns in a great game. There were to be no arms and no invasion force. 'They don't care a fig for our cause by itself,' he wrote bitterly to John Devoy in June 1915, 'they know nothing of us or it or our country … They will not help us with arms or anything.'

The failure of the Germans to support the insurrection in the way the rebels hoped left them fatally isolated on Easter Monday. But around the world the events of the following week were seen through the prism of the global turmoil. Trot-

sky described the Rising as 'this picture which history has set in the frame of the world war'. Eyewitness accounts of the Rising compared it to the trench warfare on the Western Front. New, but already iconic, images of the ravages inflicted on Ypres and Louvain were invoked to describe the ruination of central Dublin. And in significant ways coverage of the fighting and its aftermath was far more detailed and vivid than the censored accounts of the slaughter in France. The newsreel reports and photographs from Dublin in Easter Week carried a greater drama to the larger war. They also appeared exotic rather than parochial: one contemporary correspondent likened the Rising to a coup in a South American republic.

Its leaders also saw themselves in the continuum of great world events. Observing Dublin from the GPO, Joseph Plunkett is said to have reflected that it was the first time a capital city had burned since Moscow. Easter Monday was declared the first day of the new Irish Republic in a conscious echo of the French Revolution. The very nature of the modern empire, connected by the technologies which it boasted were its gift to world progress (telegraph, telephone and wireless signals, and the English language itself), made it second nature for the rebels to proclaim their achievement to the world; Ireland was an important node in this vast network. Volunteers braved

snipers' bullets to erect an aerial and repair a transmitter on the roof of the Irish School of Wireless Telegraphy near the GPO. Then James Connolly sent over a text proclaiming the Irish Republic and the taking over of Dublin by the Republican Army, which was broadcast in the hope that it would be picked up (this was later hailed by Marshall McLuhan as the first global radio broadcast). Inside the GPO the veteran Fenian Thomas Clarke roused his fighters by telling them that the awakening of national feeling in Ireland was a secondary justification for the Rising: its primary purpose was to make a timely protest so that the Irish Republic could claim recognition from the rest of the world at the peace conference that would follow an armistice.

The context in which Irish leaders pressed their claims for recognition of their nation was transformed between 1914 and 1918. When the war started, Ireland's cause could be perceived as a provincial squabble within the United Kingdom. By 1918, empires had collapsed and the world was being reordered according to the 'national principle'. New nations were springing up all over Europe: Poland, Ukraine, Finland. Buchan, a committed internationalist, was horrified: 'To allow any racial oddment to start house . . . would produce not freedom but anarchy'.

But the mass political party that emerged from the violent uprising in 1916 could now argue convincingly that limited self-government for Ireland within the United Kingdom was an anachronism. In 1917 the Sinn Féin leader Arthur Griffith wrote that it did not matter anymore that Home Rule had been approved by the British parliament, awaiting the end of the war for implementation; Ireland's gaze and ambitions had moved beyond London and what could be achieved there. 'Ireland is out of the corner where for generations she had been hidden away from the world. She is no longer an island lying behind England — she is again politically, as well as geographically, part of Europe.'

CULTURAL LEGACY

BY **ROY FOSTER**

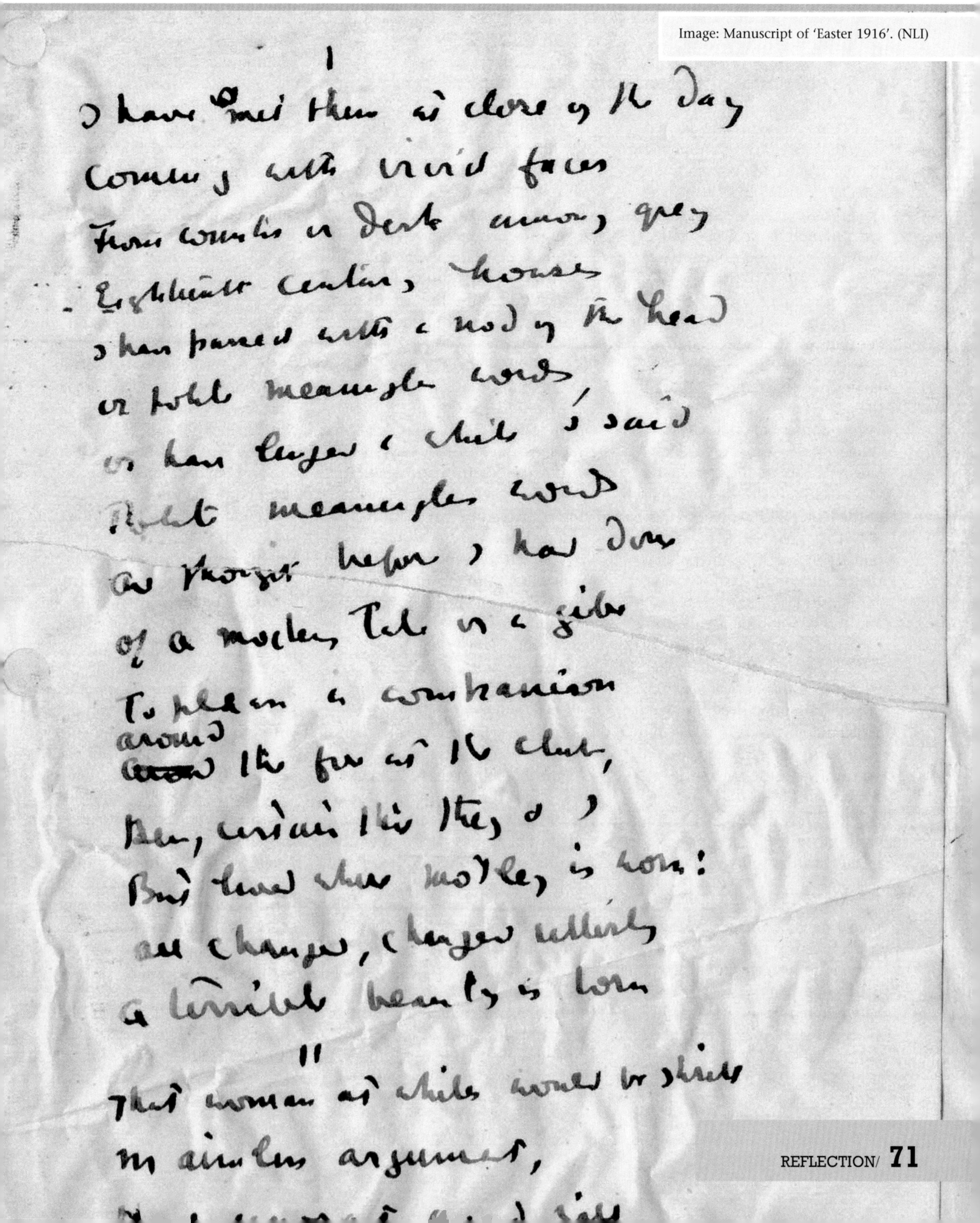

Image: Manuscript of 'Easter 1916'. (NLI)

I

I have met them at close of day
Coming with vivid faces
From counters or desks among grey
Eighteenth century houses
I have passed with a nod of the head
or polite meaningless words,
or have lingered awhile & said
Polite meaningless words
And thought before I had done
of a mocking tale or a gibe
To please a companion
around the fire at the club,
Being certain that they & I
But lived where motley is worn:
all changed, changed utterly
A terrible beauty is born

II

That woman as while would be shrill
In aimless argument,

Many early commentators missed the ambivalence towards the Rising that lies at the heart of the poet's 'Easter 1916'

YEATS CHANGED ONLY SLOWLY

W.B. Yeats is indelibly associated with the Easter Rising, through one famous poem. He returned to the subject in several more works, a time-travelling Noh-inspired play *The Dreaming of the Bones*, and a resonant question embedded in a chilling late poem, 'The Statues'. 'When Pearse summoned Cuchulain to his side, / What stalked through the Post Office?' (The answer, rather surprisingly, seems to be some race-memory of eugenic purity.) But it is the powerful poetic sequence 'Easter 1916', announcing that all is changed utterly and 'a terrible beauty is born', which sealed his identification with the opening act of the Irish Revolution.

This is ironic, because the underlying theme of the poem is the conflict between immovable, extremist ideas and the flux of life, and Yeats's ambivalence about the necessity of violent sacrificial action echoes through the poem. When he wrote it, he was not yet a supporter of Sinn Féin; moreover, his own personal and emotional life was in flux, as is clearly indicated in the third stanza. The Rising marked a watershed in his life, as it did in his country's history. But this became clear only slowly, a process reflected in the poem's cautious publishing history.

While the IRB inner circle were preparing their Easter *émeute*, with secret missions to Germany and elaborate stratagems to mislead their colleagues, Yeats was occupying a very different world. He was 50 years old and his early advanced-nationalist sympathies had been put behind him. The days of his involvement in Fenian-influenced 1898 centenary organisations, and his joint authorship of *Cathleen Ni Houlihan*, were far behind, though he was still capable of summoning them up when he needed to display nationalist credentials. Maud Gonne had been a central influence in this, however, and after her scandalous separation from John MacBride in 1904, and the unsupportive reaction of MacBride's IRB colleagues, Yeats had become antagonistic to advanced-nationalist circles (much more so than Gonne). Struggles over the repertoire of the Abbey Theatre, with Arthur Griffith and Sinn Féin violently attacking the representation of Ireland in Synge's plays, widened the gap.

So did the evolving pattern of Yeats's life. With growing success, he divided his time between London and summers with Lady Gregory at Coole Park; symbolically, in 1907 he felt unable to attend the funeral of his old mentor, the Fenian John O'Leary, and went to Italy with Gregory instead. He had been approached about receiving a knighthood, and wisely put a stop to the idea. By 1912 his politics were Redmondite and his attitude to republican zealots lofty and faintly derisive—as vividly indicated in the first stanza of 'Easter 1916'.

For their part, younger people of republican beliefs tended to see him as unacceptably Anglophile, and as someone who had repudiated his Revivalist past and opted for élitist art above nationalist politics.

Thus the news of the Rising broke on his head like a thunderstorm. He was staying with the artist William Rothenstein at Oakridge, Gloucestershire, and intelligence filtered in through unreliable news bulletins and letters from friends—principally his sister Lily and his closest friend, Augusta Gregory. Neither was supportive of the rebels at first. Lily was vehemently angry that all hopes of Home Rule would now be dashed; she wrote to John Quinn that the Rising was 'childish madness' and sent a mordant letter to her brother dismissing several of the principals—Constance Markievicz for her hereditary 'madness', Thomas MacDonagh as 'clever and hard and full of self-conceit', Patrick Pearse as 'a dreamer and a sentimentalist', and John MacBride as a drunk. These very people would later be memorialised by her brother in 'Easter 1916'.

Gregory's response to the Rising was more nuanced: 'my mind is filled with sorrow at the Dublin tragedy, the death of Pearse and McDonough [*sic*], who ought to have been on our side, the side of intellectual freedom … It seems as if the leaders were what is wanted in Ireland—and will be even more wanted in the future—a fearless and imaginative opposition to the conventional and opportunist parliamentarians … I wish we could have won that "enterprise and fortitude and disinterestedness" to our side.'

In these letters we can track the slow change of opinion among moderate nationalists—and the swift realisation that the policy of executions was utterly counterproductive from the British (or Home Ruler) point of view. Yeats's friend Charles Ricketts had assured him that the government's reaction would be as in 1848: 'discover that Roger Casement was insane, imprison the leaders during the war pending the investigations over the extent of German intrigues in the matter, discover that these men were misguided dupes, and probably amnesty them after the war'.

This is exactly what did not happen, and Lily's reaction was furious. 'This whole work here is so horrible I hate to write of it, this shooting of foolish idealists, not a vicious man among them except perhaps MacBride, Maud Gonne's husband.' A little later she wrote that the Rising and its aftermath might be 'the beginning of Ireland'.

As Yeats absorbed these seismic events and the changing reactions to them, and ruminated on Maud Gonne's remark to him that 'tragic dignity had returned to Ireland', he began to think about writing a poem on the subject. He hesitated to visit Dublin, but he finally arrived in May and was shocked at the ruination of the city and the toxic political atmosphere after the executions. Moreover, one of those executions carried particular import for him: with MacBride's death, Maud Gonne was now a widow. Instead of heading for Coole, Yeats departed for Gonne's summer house on the beach at Colleville, in Normandy (now Omaha Beach). He went there with the intention of proposing marriage to her, as he informed a rather sceptical Gregory. He did so, and was refused. But during his sojourn there he found himself more and more drawn to Gonne's beautiful but neurotic 22-year-old daughter Iseult; he would propose to her and be refused in turn.

And all through the summer he was working on the poem that became 'Easter 1916', completed in September.

Gonne would long afterwards remember his staying up all night to complete the poem, and afterwards asking her to marry him one more time. 'He implored me to forget the stone and its inner fire for the flashing, changing joy of life, but … he found my mind dull with the stone of the fixed idea of getting back to Ireland.' This is a conflation; he actually finished the poem at Coole Park, not Colleville, and his journey back from France with her happened the following summer. But the emphasis on the conflict of ideas in the poem is salient, with the rush of images suggesting the sensual, fulfilling world of love, procreation and running water, swirling around the idea of fixed, immovable opinions and what he elsewhere

called (in relation to Pearse) 'the vertigo of self-sacrifice'.

When the poem was completed at Coole, he sent it to Gonne and it was fiercely debated in the Normandy house by the sea, as Iseult rapidly informed him. 'Your poem on the Easter week has been the cause of great argument in our household as to the nature and value of sacrifice. Moura [Gonne] who cannot admit Art for art's sake would willingly admit sacrifice for sacrifice's sake, and I have come to admit neither exactly.' Maud herself made her feelings clear, in a letter

that goes to the heart of the poem's ambiguity:

'No I don't like your poem, it isn't worthy of you and above all it isn't worthy of the subject— Though it reflects your present state of mind perhaps, it isn't quite sincere enough for you who have studied philosophy and know something of history know

●

Above: Major John McBride is marched to his court martial. 'This other man I had dreamed / A drunken, vainglorious lout'. (Kilmainham Gaol Museum 17PD-IAI4-23)

quite well that sacrifice has never yet turned a heart to stone though it has immortalised many and through it alone mankind can rise to God … you could never say that MacDonagh and Pearse and Conally [sic] were sterile fixed minds, each served Ireland, which was their share of the world, the part they were in contact with, with varied faculties and vivid energy! Those three were men of genius with large comprehensive and speculative and active brains[;] the others of whom we know less were probably less remarkable men, but still I think they must have been men with a stronger grasp on Reality[,] a stronger spiritual life than most of those we meet. As for my husband he has entered Eternity by the great door of sacrifice which Christ opened and has therefore atoned for all so that praying for him I can also ask for his prayers and "A terrible beauty is born".'

Less perceptive readers would take 'Easter 1916' as a straight endorsement of the rebels and their cause, and, as it found its way into circulation, this is certainly how it was interpreted. Yeats's own sympathies were moving toward the Sinn Féin cause, but cautiously. Though he described the rebels as 'the ablest and most fine natured of our young men', his relations with the survivors were not close and Griffith was an old enemy. Yeats campaigned for clemency for Roger Casement, wrote powerful letters opposing the introduction of conscription for Ireland, and condemned the British rule of Ireland in private. But his first public declaration of support for Sinn Féin and denunciation of British policy in Ireland would be in early 1920, at the Oxford Union, spurred by his horror at Black-and-Tan atrocities around Galway.

In 1916–17 he had strong reasons for caution in publishing a pro-rebel poem. One may have been his reliance on a Literary Fund pension, but the principal reason involved the campaign that he and Gregory were simultaneously mounting, dedicated to reclaiming Hugh Lane's great Impressionist paintings for Ireland. The collection had been left to found the nucleus of a modern art gallery in Dublin by a codicil drawn up by Lane, but not witnessed, just prior to his death on board the *Lusitania* in 1915. While it was generally admitted that this was his intention, the National Gallery in London claimed them under an earlier will, and Gregory and Yeats were pulling every political string they could to get this decision rescinded. Their chief supporter in the government was the Unionist

Left: A 1904 National Theatre poster advertising plays by Lady Gregory, Yeats and Synge. Yeats had become antagonistic to advanced-nationalist circles, in part owing to struggles over the repertoire, with Arthur Griffith and Sinn Féin violently attacking the representation of Ireland in Synge's plays. (National Library of Ireland)

leader Edward Carson, and Yeats was acutely conscious that the publication of a rebel poem would have immediate repercussions for the cause of the Lane pictures. This point was strongly made by Gregory, he recorded, 'and she is not timid'.

By 1920 things would look very different, and Gregory's opinions had also become much more frankly republican (she would remain more 'advanced' on this issue than Yeats, as did his brother Jack). The poem would eventually be published in October 1920 in the *New Statesman*—a journal that was campaigning strongly on behalf of Terence MacSwiney, then on hunger strike. (This was another reason why the ambiguity of the poem was not much noticed by its early interpreters.) Up to then, it had circulated in a sort of *samizdat* fashion: Clement Shorter printed a limited pamphlet edition, and Yeats read it to private gatherings. But he kept it out of his 1919 collection *The Wild Swans at Coole*, though it made a ghostly appearance on an early, abandoned, draft of the title-page. The canonical version would appear in *Michael Robartes and the Dancer* (1921), along with more unequivocally 'rebel' poems such as 'The Rose Tree' and 'Sixteen Dead Men'.

By the time it was published in 1920, too, much had 'changed utterly' in Yeats's personal life. The emotional roller-coaster of 1916–17, and his involvement with the Gonnes, had left him very near a nervous breakdown; in September 1917, in a state of considerable *Sturm und Drang*, he had proposed to George Hyde-Lees, who, at 25, was nearly as young as Iseult. They married on 20 October and after a rocky beginning, overcome by joint psychic explorations, Yeats found

● Above right: W.B. Yeats: 'The news of the Rising broke on his head like a thunderstorm'. (National Library of Ireland)

● Right: Gregory's response to the Rising was more nuanced: 'my mind is filled with sorrow at the Dublin tragedy, the death of Pearse and McDonough [*sic*], who ought to have been on our side, the side of intellectual freedom'. (National Library of Ireland)

Easter 1916

I have met them at close of day
Coming with vivid faces
From counter or desk among grey
Eighteenth-century houses.
I have passed with a nod of the head
Or polite meaningless words,
Or have lingered awhile and said
Polite meaningless words,
And thought before I had done
Of a mocking tale or a gibe
To please a companion
Around the fire at the club,
Being certain that they and I
But lived where motley is worn:
All changed, changed utterly:
A terrible beauty is born.

That woman's days were spent
In ignorant good-will,
Her nights in argument
Until her voice grew shrill.
What voice more sweet than hers
When, young and beautiful,
She rode to harriers?
This man had kept a school
And rode our wingèd horse;
This other his helper and friend
Was coming into his force;
He might have won fame in the end,
So sensitive his nature seemed,
So daring and sweet his thought.
This other man I had dreamed
A drunken, vainglorious lout.
He had done most bitter wrong
To some who are near my heart,
Yet I number him in the song;
He, too, has resigned his part
In the casual comedy;
He, too, has been changed in his turn,
Transformed utterly:
A terrible beauty is born.

Hearts with one purpose alone
Through summer and winter seem
Enchanted to a stone
To trouble the living stream.
The horse that comes from the road,
The rider, the birds that range
From cloud to tumbling cloud,
Minute by minute they change;
A shadow of cloud on the stream
Changes minute by minute;
A horse-hoof slides on the brim,
And a horse plashes within it;
The long-legged moor-hens dive,
And hens to moor-cocks call;
Minute by minute they live;
The stone's in the midst of all.

Too long a sacrifice
Can make a stone of the heart.
O when may it suffice?
That is Heaven's part, our part
To murmur name upon name,
As a mother names her child
When sleep at last has come
On limbs that had run wild.
What is it but nightfall?
No, no, not night but death;
Was it needless death after all?
For England may keep faith
For all that is done and said.
We know their dream; enough
To know they dreamed and are dead;
And what if excess of love
Bewildered them till they died?
I write it out in a verse —
MacDonagh and MacBride
And Connolly and Pearse
Now and in time to be,
Wherever green is worn,
Are changed, changed utterly:
A terrible beauty is born.

25 September 1916

From Michael Robartes and the Dancer (1921) Macmillan

When he wrote it, Yeats was not yet a supporter of Sinn Féin; moreover, his own personal and emotional life was in flux, as is clearly indicated in the third stanza.

Thus 1916 began a period of turmoil and change for him, in his political and emotional life, and the poem takes its rise from that. It also derives its power from a sense of agonised uncertainty that pulses through the stanzas; this is not altogether resolved by the beautiful and reconciliatory images of sleep, death and the telling of names that bring about a conclusion. It remains, along with 'Parnell's Funeral' sixteen years later, Yeats's most resonant political poem. And it raises questions that are still being asked in the year of the 1916 centenary.

●

Below: The library at Coole Park, home of Lady Gregory, where 'Easter 1916' was composed. (Colin Smythe)

himself rescued into serenity. From 1918 the Yeatses began spending summers in Galway, renovating their tower-house at Ballylee, near Coole; they would move back to Dublin during the Civil War, and Yeats would become a senator and 'smiling public man' in the new Free State.

Since the summer of 1916 he had been wondering about returning to Ireland to 'begin building again', strongly encouraged by Gregory: 'there must be some spiritual building possible just as after Parnell's fall, but perhaps more intense and you have a big name among the young men'.

CHURCH REACTION

BY **BRIAN P. MURPHY, OSM**

Image: Joseph Mary Plunkett and Grace Gifford, who married in Kilmainham Gaol the evening before his execution. When on Holy Saturday Plunkett had told Eoin MacNeill that 'the pope had sent his blessing to the Irish Volunteers' and to himself in particular, MacNeill declared that he 'was then ready to take part in the rising'. Yet only hours later, when he read of the failure to land arms in Kerry, he changed his mind. (Illustration by David Rooney from *1916: portraits and lives* (Royal Irish Academy, 2015))

Bishop O'Dwyer's immediate and cogent defence of the Rising has been too long ignored

LIMERICK'S REBEL PRELATE

In short, the terms of the just rebellion theory did not apply to Ireland: they applied to a sovereign state with a tyrannical ruler and not to a nation conquered by an imperial power

The members of the Irish Republican Brotherhood (IRB) responsible for the Rising had two good reasons to be aware of the moral issues regarding plans for a rebellion. First, they were acutely aware that, as a secret society formed, as the Fenian Brotherhood, in 1858 to end British rule in Ireland, they had been excommunicated by Pope Pius IX in 1870, and that his successor, Pope Leo XIII, had condemned the Plan of Campaign in 1888. Second, some members of the IRB had been specifically informed by Eoin MacNeill, the president of the Irish Volunteers, that a rebellion was not morally justified. These instructions of MacNeill's, drawn up and delivered in mid-February 1916, not only had an effect on the IRB's actions leading up to the Rising but also later became a significant influence on the debate about the morality of the Rising when they were published by F. X. Martin in *Irish Historical Studies* in 1961.

While plans went ahead for a rising, an initiative was also undertaken to ease MacNeill's moral qualms: Count Plunkett, the father of Joseph Mary Plunkett, was sent on a mission to Rome in early April to secure the approval of Pope Benedict XV (elected September 1914) for a blessing on the Irish Volunteers. In the days immediately prior to the Rising, MacNeill changed his mind almost daily with regard to its legitimacy. Significantly, when on Holy

After the Easter Rising, one of the first public statements to mention it with reference to the just rebellion theory appeared as soon as June in *The Month*, a Jesuit journal published in England. It declared that 'the Dublin revolt to all unprejudiced eyes lacked the first elements of justification. Morality countenances rebellion only as the act of a grievously oppressed people who have no constitutional means of redress, and who may reasonably hope for success through this means.'

The author then enunciated three ways in which the Rising failed to meet the above criteria: first, it was the work of a small group of people who did not represent the views of the majority; second, it took place when constitutional reform was taking place; third, the rebels had no rational ground for expecting success.

The debate over these principles has been running since the Rising to the present day. Let us examine these moral principles in the light of the political situation of the time, and—especially—with regard to the role of the pope and the Irish presence at Rome.

Saturday, 22 April, he was informed
by Joseph Mary Plunkett that 'the
pope had sent his blessing to the
Irish Volunteers' and to himself in
particular, MacNeill declared that he
'was then ready to take part in the
rising'. Yet only hours later, when he
read of the failure to land arms in
Kerry, he changed his mind.

While it is perhaps too fanciful
to suggest that the IRB was influenced by the opinion of Fr George
Crolly (1813–78), a former professor
at Maynooth, who had suggested—
decades earlier—that a rebellion
could never be justified unless the
rebels had secured the approval of
the pope, the connection with Rome
provides a valuable insight into the
debate on the morality of the Rising.

Mgr O'Riordain, rector of the
Irish College in Rome from 1905
until his death in 1919, played a
central role in influencing Bishop
O'Dwyer's attitude towards the First
World War and the Rising. He had
arranged Count Plunkett's meeting
with the pope on 8 April at which
the blessing on the Volunteers had
been given: a blessing, it should be
noted, that was neither on the IRB
nor on the Rising itself. Remarkably,
in 1905 O'Riordain had arranged a
similar meeting of John Redmond
with Pope Pius X, at which the pope
had expressed, in writing, his wish
that Redmond might 'win that
liberty which makes for the welfare
of the whole country'. Clearly
O'Riordain had frequent access to the

pope and was, obviously, in regular
contact with his own superior,
Bishop Edward O'Dwyer.

O'Dwyer, therefore, knew well
the actions of Sir Henry Howard and
Cardinal Gasquet to win the pope
over to the British side in the war.
Howard's appointment as English
special envoy in December 1914 had
been privately supported by John
Redmond. Most significantly, through
O'Riordain, Bishop O'Dwyer knew
the terms of the secret London Treaty
(26 April 1915) between the Entente
powers and Italy, which stated, in
Article XV, that representatives of the
Holy See would not be allowed 'to
take any diplomatic steps for the
conclusion of peace or in regard to
matters pertaining to the present
war'. It was against this background
that Bishop O'Dwyer publicly criticised Redmond for not responding to
the pope's many pleas for peace.

Bishop O'Dwyer's justification
of the Easter Rising on moral grounds
was made on 14 September 1916 in a
speech to mark his acceptance of the
Freedom of the City of Limerick.
Previously, on 17 May 1916, immediately after the execution of fifteen
men and the deportation of many
others without civil process, he had
informed General Maxwell that 'your
regime has been one of the worst and
blackest chapters in the history of the

misgovernment of this country'. In
his September speech Bishop
O'Dwyer declared that 'the Irish
Volunteers were too few for the
enterprise, but that, perhaps, is the
worst that can be said against them.
Rebellion to be lawful must be the
act of a nation as a whole,' he continued, 'but while that is true … I
should like to ask Mr Asquith if the
destruction of the Irish Parliament
was not an atrocious crime against
this country and if as a nation we
have ever condoned or forfeited our
right to redress.' In that context,
O'Dwyer argued, persuasively and
ironically, that 'these Irish Volunteers
imagined that Ireland had an inalien-
able right to govern herself: that the
deprivation of it was worse for every
interest of their country … that it
was a usurpation, and that resistance
to it was a duty. Of course they were
wrong (laughter). These reasons
might hold good against any other
country, but not against England, the
home of freedom, the chivalrous and
disinterested friend everywhere of
small nationalities that take her side
(laughter and applause).' In short, the
terms of the just rebellion theory did
not apply to Ireland: they applied to
a sovereign state with a tyrannical
ruler and not to a nation that had
been conquered by an imperial
power.

Above: Edward Carson (with James Craig to his left) signing the Solemn League and Covenant in September 1912. That event was one of several, including the Curragh Mutiny and the Larne gunrunning to arm the Ulster Volunteers, which led Patrick Pearse to abandon a Home Rule policy and to embrace revolution. (National Library of Ireland)

Bishop O'Dwyer made this point more succinctly in his private correspondence with Bishop Patrick Foley of Kildare and Leighlin on 14 December 1916. Citing the recent works of three Jesuits—Joseph Endive, Auguste Castelein and Joseph Rickaby—as well as Fr Crolly and other authorities, O'Dwyer stated that 'the English Parliament in Ireland is a usurpation, and, having regard to the modern development of the idea of nationality and its rights, I would hold that, *positis ponendis* [taking everything into account], it would justify revolt'. The views of Bishop O'Dwyer had evolved significantly since he had aligned himself with Pope Leo XIII in the 1880s and become known as a 'Castle' bishop—that is, one who supported the British Dublin Castle administration.

Remarkably, one of the few people to make a similar distinction at the time was Lenin, who, writing in July 1916, defended the right of small nations to assert their right to self-determination against an imperial power. In regard to Ireland, he was aware of the socialist dimension of the Rising and he observed that 'a blow delivered against British imperialist bourgeois rule by a rebellion in Ireland is of a hundred times greater political significance than a blow of equal weight in Asia or in Africa'.

The views of Bishop O'Dwyer, however, had no public support from members of the hierarchy, and several of them, including Cardinal Logue and Archbishop Harty of Cashel, made statements condemning the Rising. Some of them did indict the rebels on the grounds of the just rebellion theory, but no public reply was made to Bishop O'Dwyer's speech in September 1916. Most of the bishops remained silent. Indeed, some of them were official supporters of Redmond's party, although by 1916 many had become more critical of Ireland's participation in the war.

While the views of Bishop O'Dwyer were gaining wide publicity, Mgr O'Riordain was not only publishing them in Rome but also writing his own justification of the Rising. His book *La recente insurrezione en Irlanda* appeared in September 1916. One copy, bound in white, was presented to the pope. O'Riordain cited extensively from the evidence to the Royal Commission of Augustine Birrell, the chief secretary, which had been very critical of the armed opposition to Home Rule by the Ulster Volunteers. He concluded that the Irish Volunteers were 'not a seditious and revolutionary force, which could be condemned out of

Alfred O'Rahilly, the noted academic, president of University College Cork and a TD for Cork City, maintained in the *Catholic Bulletin* in September 1916 that *'to condemn an uprising merely on the grounds of the consequent loss of life and property, would betray a singular blindness to the spiritual realities of life'*.

hand by Catholic theology'.

In his argument, some of the following events, which led Pearse to abandon a Home Rule policy and to embrace revolution, were mentioned: the Ulster Covenant to resist the Home Rule Bill by force (September 1912); the Ulster Provisional Government (September 1913); the Curragh Mutiny; the Larne gunrunning to arm the Ulster Volunteers; the Defence of the Realm Act, which placed Ireland under martial law; the threat of Sir Edward Carson to resist the Home Rule Act by force (all 1914); and the appointment of Carson and other Tory MPs, who had supported armed resistance to Home Rule, as members of a Coalition War Cabinet (1915).

Like Bishop O'Dwyer, O'Riordain saw the promise of Home Rule as 'a trap in order to enlist Irishmen' into the British army, and he then compared the Easter Rising to the conflict over Belgium. He argued that if the British had a right to military intervention in Belgium because Germany had torn up a treaty as 'a scrap of paper', then the Irish had good reason to take armed action against England because it, too, had torn up the Home Rule Act like 'a scrap of paper'.

The opinions of Bishop O'Dwyer and Mgr O'Riordain on the morality of the Easter Rising are of great significance: if, as they argued, there is a difference between a usurping power and a tyrannical power, then objections based on the classic principles of a just rebellion simply did not apply. Alfred O'Rahilly, writing at the same time as these churchmen, agreed, and he added that it was also reasonable to rebel even if there was little hope of success. O'Rahilly had tried his vocation as a Jesuit from 1901 to 1914 and had a profound knowledge of scholastic moral teaching. Writing in the *Catholic Bulletin* in September 1916, and having reflected on the example of the Christian martyrs, O'Rahilly maintained that 'to condemn an uprising merely on the grounds of the consequent loss of life and property, would betray a singular blindness to the spiritual realities of life'. He then cited a Catholic *Primer of peace and war* to the effect that 'a protest against injustice is always valuable even if not actually successful and no protest is more emphatic than that made by preferring death to submission'. He concluded with the words of the poet Milton:

'the greatest gift the hero leaves his race
 Is to have been a hero. Say we fail!
 We feed the high tradition of the world,

And leave our spirit in our children's breasts.'

Subsequent events, especially the ever-increasing horror of the war and the passing of a Conscription Act on Ireland in April 1918, led to what might be called a *post factum* approval of the ideals of the Easter Rising by all political parties. Gathered in the Mansion House on 18 April 1918, Éamon de Valera and Arthur Griffith, representing Sinn Féin, joined with John Dillon and Joseph Devlin, representing the Irish Party, together with representatives from Labour and other parties, and declared that 'the passing of the Conscription Bill by the British House of Commons must be regarded as a declaration of war on the Irish nation … it is in direct violation of the rights of small nationalities to self-determination'. The declaration was immediately endorsed by the Roman Catholic hierarchy, and articles in June 1918 by Fr Peter Coffey (*Irish Ecclesiastical Record*) and Fr Peter Finlay SJ (*Studies*) advanced a theology of resistance to British rule in Ireland. Finlay's article relied on many of the sources which had fashioned the reasoning of Bishop O'Dwyer, and his thinking was reflected in the Proclamations of Dáil Éireann in January 1921, although O'Dwyer had died earlier, on 19 August 1917.

The intellectual rationale which O'Dwyer had enunciated to justify the Easter Rising was, however, ignored by Fr Walter McDonald, a former professor at Maynooth, in his 1919 book *Some ethical questions of peace and war*, and has not been adverted to in the historical reappraisal of the Easter Rising which has taken place since the 1966 anniversary. Central to that debate has been the publication by F.X. Martin of Eoin MacNeill's memoir in 1961, mentioned at the start of this article, an article by Fr Francis Shaw in *Studies* (1972), the writings of Conor Cruise O'Brien and Garret FitzGerald, and, most recently, an article by John Bruton in *Studies* (autumn 2014). In varying degrees these authors have condemned the Rising as unjustified.

The voices of Bishop O'Dwyer and Mgr O'Riordain tell a different story of the causes of the Easter Rising: a story that gives fitting prominence to the actions of Ulster and Tory Unionists; a story that exposes the duplicity of British war aims; and a story that provides a new insight into the morality of the Rising. For all of these reasons, the words of Bishop O'Dwyer that 'the English Parliament in Ireland is a usurpation' and that 'it would justify revolt' merit attention and debate.

Further reading

J. aan de Wiel, *The Catholic Church in Ireland, 1914–1918* (Dublin, 2003).

J.A. Gaughan, *Alfred O'Rahilly, vol. II: public figure* (Dublin, 1989).

D. Keogh, *The Vatican, the bishops and Irish politics, 1919–1939* (Cambridge, 1986).

A. McGrath, 'The Anglo-Irish War (1919–1921): just war or unjust rebellion?', *Irish Theological Quarterly* **77** (1) (2012).

T.J. Morrissey SJ, *Bishop Edward Thomas O'Dwyer of Limerick, 1842–1917* (Dublin, 2003).

B.P. Murphy OSB, *The Catholic Bulletin and Republican Ireland* (Belfast, 2005).

●

Below: F. X. Martin: In February 1916 Eoin MacNeill had formally informed members of the IRB that a rebellion could not be morally justified. Fr Martin's publication, in 1961, of this memoir helped to launch a historical reappraisal of the Rising. (Thaddeus Breen)

PEARSE
DENOUNCED

BY **JOE LEE**

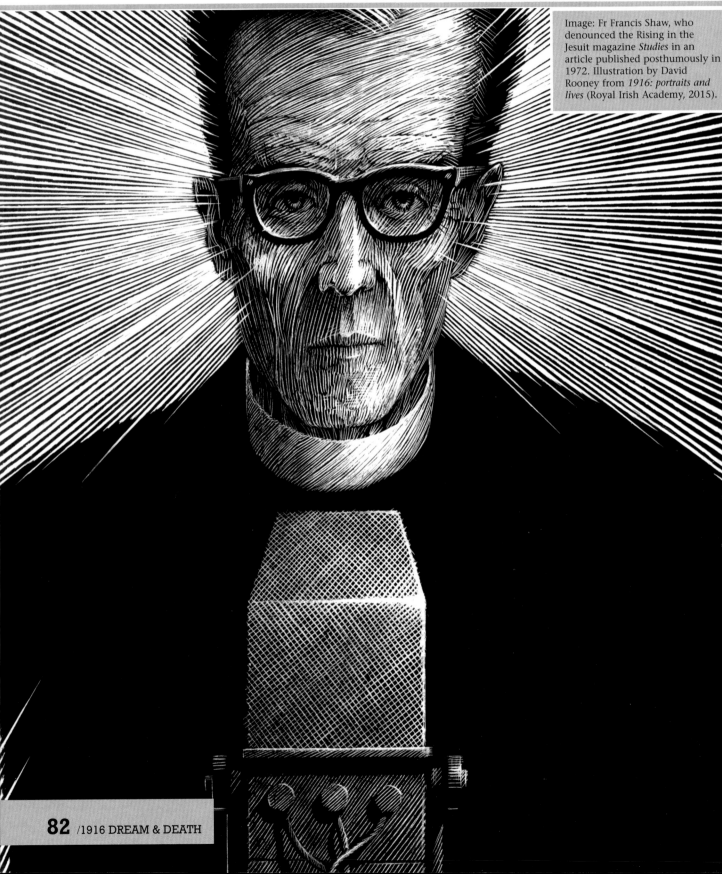

Image: Fr Francis Shaw, who denounced the Rising in the Jesuit magazine *Studies* in an article published posthumously in 1972. Illustration by David Rooney from *1916: portraits and lives* (Royal Irish Academy, 2015).

In a battle of polemicists, the tedious search for evidence is the first victim

DON'T LET FACTS RUIN A GOOD ARGUMENT

The manner in which Pearse is quoted in historical writing offers a litmus test of the intellectual integrity as well as the intellectual calibre of the writer.

Fr Francis Shaw's celebrated denunciation of the 1916 Rising, and particularly of Patrick Pearse, published posthumously in Vol. 61 of the Jesuit journal *Studies* ('The canon of Irish history: a challenge') in 1972, begins promisingly from a historian's perspective. He denounces Pearse's interpretation of Irish history as 'a straight story of black and white, of good guys and bad. The truth of course is different: there are many qualifications and complexities, and this essay is concerned with some of them.' The historian, of course, revels in 'qualifications and complexities', as that is what so much of life is about.

Sadly, 'qualifications and complexities' are what Fr Shaw's own essay singularly lacks. There is simply a reversal, indeed more than a reversal, of 'good guys and bad'—'more than a reversal' because his way of dealing with James Connolly and the Citizen Army is breathtaking in its disdain for historical scholarship. Connolly and his followers are swept not only out of 1916 but also virtually out of Irish history in one dismissive sentence (p. 119)—but not, apparently, out of world history. For Fr Shaw, the Citizen Army can be omitted 'because basically it is more a part of world history than of Irish history'.

However striking an exercise of mental and verbal gymnastics this may be, what does it actually mean? How can something happening in Ireland be part of world history but so much less a part of Irish history that it can be evicted? Can Ireland step in and step out—or be stepped

in and out—of 'world history' as ideological convenience dictates? How much else of Irish history can be conveniently eliminated from domestic consideration by relegating it to world history, whatever exactly that is deemed to be? Is Ireland not part of the world? Are the members of the Citizen Army not just as Irish as Fr Shaw or any of the rest of us? What mind-set lurks behind so dismissive an attitude?

Connolly, quite a dogmatist himself, might even be tempted to claim that it vindicated his socialist perspective, for how could anything else be expected from so quintessential a product of 'a leading Mullingar business dynasty' (Patrick Maume, 'Francis Shaw 1907–70', in L.W. White and J. Quinn (eds), *1916: portraits and lives* (Dublin, 2015), p. 293)? At the very least, the thought process behind this arbitrary eviction of Connolly from Irish history to 'world history' requires clarification.

Having thus evicted Connolly from Irish history to his satisfaction, Fr Shaw trains his polemical guns on Pearse. Fr Shaw is a formidable polemicist, and Pearse is an inviting target. But in his enthusiasm to identify examples of Pearse cutting corners, Fr Shaw invites analysis of his own performance in this regard. Consider his assertion that 'in 1914 an armed soldiery stood between Ireland and its destiny'. This is a rather curious formulation. The only 'destiny' on the table at that juncture was Home Rule. Why was Home Rule its destiny? Who has so decreed? Is this written on some hitherto concealed tablet of stone?

But leaving this aside, who is

this 'armed soldiery'? Fr Shaw was at pains to emphasise that it was not the British army but the Ulster Volunteer Force. This might suggest to the unwary that the British army were neutral observers in the determination of Ireland's destiny. This formulation, however, makes it look as if Fr Shaw had never heard of the Curragh Mutiny of 1914 in which the British officer corps effectively determined that the British army would not move against the UVF. Partition, even if the details remained to be determined, was therefore inevitable. In the context it is simply a distortion to refer to 'the considerable degree of self-determination for 32 counties that was being offered them in 1914' (p. 122).

Part of the intemperate phraseology of some of Fr Shaw's argument seems to derive from his indignation at the idea of there being any final arbiter of Irish destiny other than Catholic churchmen. 'Irishmen of today are invited at least implicitly to apologise for their fellow-countrymen who accepted loyally the serious guidance of the church to which they belonged' (p. 119). It would seem that Protestants have suddenly vanished from Ireland in what is apparently an internal argument between Catholics.

'In the commonly accepted view of Irish history', we are told, the Irishman of today is asked to disown his past. He is expected to censure as unpatriotic the common Irishmen who were not attracted by the new revolutionary ideas but who adhered to an ancient tradition. The chronology here is so vague that it is difficult to engage in detailed analysis of the assumptions about Irish history underlying it, except that Fr Shaw

Above: Perhaps it was Patrick Pearse's training in law which made him a brilliant polemicist. Nevertheless, he 'strove to keep (his) options open sufficiently—even down to his final tribute, in his last GPO dispatch, to Eoin MacNeill, Fr Shaw's hero—to make it unpredictable where he might have stood, at least in principle, on the most divisive issues after 1916'. (National Library of Ireland)

appears to cherish an image of an all but omnipotent Catholic Church as the dominant political power, no less than religious power, in Ireland, an image that would gladden the hearts of its most bitter critics.

The thought processes and methodologies of Pearse and Fr Shaw actually had much in common, horrified though both might be to hear it. There is a striking similarity between their methodologies. Both largely dispense with the vulgarity of evidence in deference to the primacy of ideologically driven assertion. Few, if any, pages are polluted by a footnote, though Pearse does include qualifications to his numerous sweeping metallic generalisations in some of his texts. Rather, the preferred style of both is to move from assertion to assertion, imposing their own ideological convictions on the motivations of the living and dead generations, substituting apparently revealed truth for the tedium of a search for evidence. Truth is what happens to suit their ideological convictions, wherever those convictions derive from in terms of intellect, education, genes or class.

Neither appears to have much concept of the use of evidence as understood by professional historians. Both are brilliant polemicists, moving from assertion to assertion apparently in the serene conviction that they are speaking revealed truth, though Pearse changes his mind sufficiently often for him to sense that he needs to provide some explanation of his policy shifts from 1912 onwards while purporting to keep to a straight line, which could lead him into awkward gymnastics to explain his shift from cultural to revolutionary nationalism. He strove to keep options open sufficiently—even down to his final tribute, in his last GPO dispatch, to Eoin MacNeill, Fr Shaw's hero—to make it unpredictable where he might have stood, at least in principle, on the most divisive issues after 1916.

Fr Shaw is confident that 'Following the lead of Tone and the Fenians Pearse, one feels, would not have been satisfied to attain independence by peaceful means. He had clearly come to believe that the purgation of blood-letting was necessary.' But 'one feels' is not a concept of evidence acceptable to the historian. The manner in which Pearse is quoted in historical writing offers a litmus test of the intellectual integrity as well as the intellectual calibre of the writer. His declamatory style lent itself to quotation out of context, an opportunity too tempting not to be eagerly seized by denigrators frequently choosing to ignore Pearse's own qualifications. As a practised polemicist, Pearse can scarcely complain. He frequently imposed a highly selective view on historical evidence, even on the limited amount available at the time. But then he did not enjoy the years of repose, or the access to historical sources, that retrospective commentators enjoy—or at least can enjoy if they are concerned with historical truth instead of knowing the answers before they begin—and who can claim no such excuse. As late as February 1916 he defended one of his heroes, Thomas Davis, against the accusation of physical-force zealots that Davis was not an unqualified advocate of rebellion with the rebuke:

'That Davis would have achieved Irish nationhood by peaceful means if he could is undoubted. Let it not be a reproach against Davis. Obviously if a nation can obtain its freedom without bloodshed, it is its duty so to obtain it. Those of us who believe that, in the circumstances of Ireland, it is not possible to obtain our freedom without bloodshed will admit thus [sic] much. If England, after due pressure, were to say to us, "Here, take Ireland", no one would be so foolish as to answer, "No, we'd rather fight you for it". But things like that do not happen. One must fight, or at least be ready to fight.'

Fr Shaw concludes his invigorating essay with an interpretation of Irish history, 'After 1916', that, although presented with an *ex cathedra* confidence, is based on so many debatable assertions—characteristically, as indeed with Pearse, presented in the guise of self-evident truths—that it would require a detailed exegesis to assess its scholarly, as distinct from polemical, value. To take a simple example, he asserts that in 1918 'the last straw was the threat of conscription. Two hundred thousand Irishmen might go voluntarily to fight with Britain, but not twenty would go as conscripts, because in that unwritten, inarticulate but very real sense of Irish nationhood the right of Britain to conscript Irishmen was never acknowledged' (pp 149–50). A historian may deem it dangerous to pronounce with such unqualified assurance on the unquestionable validity of an 'unwritten, inarticulate' source, but leaving aside the pedantic, if valid, observation that the figure of 200,000 can only be arrived at by conscripting many Ulster unionists into Sinn Féiners in 1918, it is far from clear that conscription could not have been successfully imposed in Ireland as in Britain in 1916. At the very least, the figure of 'not twenty' must be treated as simply a figure of speech.

It comes, too, as something of

Right: A First World War recruitment poster. The Irish were encouraged to enlist, as Home Rule awaited only the end of the war. Fr Shaw insists that in 1914 Home Rule was Ireland's 'destiny'. Was it?

Below right: Members of Connolly's Irish Citizen Army outside Liberty Hall. Fr Shaw's 'way of dealing with James Connolly and the Citizen Army is breathtaking in its disdain for historical scholarship. Connolly and his followers are swept not only out of 1916 but virtually out of Irish history in one dismissive sentence'. (National Library of Ireland)

a surprise to learn that, 'in the important matter of electoral reform', 'Ireland in 1916 was a democracy' (p. 146), an assertion which might provoke the suspicion that women, together with the poorest category of men, neither of whom had the vote, did not feature prominently in Fr Shaw's concept of either Irish history or democracy. He can talk of the historical record between the end of the Famine and 1916 without adverting to post-Famine Ireland's unrivalled achievement in actually reducing its population significantly over that period (p. 146). His mindset is instinctively partitionist, despite his reference to the wound of partition (p. 151). It has no place for the growth of Belfast in the record of Irish achievement since the Famine.

His instincts would appear to be—not surprisingly, given his social and ideological background—those of the cosy middle class. His depiction of the role of emigration in post-Famine history (p. 152) is a travesty of the reality of power relationships both between social classes and within families, reflecting allegedly 'a will to cling to the land which had given them so little, even when half had to leave so that the other half could remain and survive'. The half who had to leave had to get out because there was no place for them in the property inheritance stakes. They had to leave not 'so that the other half could remain and survive' but so that they themselves could survive.

Fr Shaw's last few pages try to pack so much in that it would be unfair to begin deconstructing them

Left: Following the Rising, the deaths of Volunteers and the execution of their leaders were frequently memorialised in a number of different ways. This memorial plaque remembers those who died and those left behind to grieve and carry on the rebellion. But Shaw felt that 'the events of 1916 and of the years which followed did close a chapter in a long history of strife, and it is time that we as a Christian people should forget the past'. (National Library of Ireland)

without clarifying the context in a degree of detail that could rival the length of his own polemic. I will pluck only a few threads from the tapestry of the peroration (p. 153).

'Ireland and Britain are two islands placed by God's creation beside one another. The paths of their respective histories have of necessity constantly crossed: in a sense they have always got in one another's way, and their relationship throughout the centuries has not been happy.' This is a curious formulation, dumping all responsibility for strife 'of necessity' on God's myopia. For one thing, they haven't 'constantly crossed', any more than the histories of neighbouring countries in Europe or elsewhere 'have constantly crossed'. Of course there has been frequent conflict between neighbours, but the intensity and duration have varied greatly, and it seems a shade harsh to dump the entire responsibility on 'God's creation'. And the crossings that occurred were due fundamentally to historical power relationships, the geographical ones being merely ways to historical ends.

Nor would one necessarily guess from Fr Shaw's bizarre formulation that the power relationship between the two islands gave rise to preponderantly one-way traffic. And they have not 'always' got in one another's way, any more than many next-door neighbours in European history have, even if it lasted far longer than average in the English/British–Irish case.

'In fact', Fr Shaw proceeds, 'the events of 1916 and of the years which followed did close a chapter in a long history of strife, and it is time that we as a Christian people should forget the past.' While one could not, of course, predict a resumption of historic conflicts, this still seems a curious conclusion to such a sustained polemic, if a perfectly logical one for the victors in the division of the spoils. A mere historian may be forgiven for dissenting, when the whole justification for the subject is not only to remember the past but also to try to understand as objectively as possible how it really was—in the still fundamental formulation of Ranke, probably the most famous of all injunctions in historical studies, *wie es eigentlich gewesen*—and to learn from it.

Of course, given human nature, complete understanding of the human condition will never be achieved—but for the historian to give up trying would be to concede defeat in one of the fundamental challenges confronting humanity.

MORAL JUSTIFICATION?

COMPILED AND EDITED BY **JOE CULLEY**

Image: Dr Edmund J. McWeeney inspecting a copy of the 1916 Proclamation on railings at St Stephen's Green, Dublin. (National Library)

The leaders knew that they had no chance of military success. How could they possibly justify their actions?

HEROIC SACRIFICE OR CRIMINAL BEHAVIOUR?

On Easter Monday, 6 April 2015, as part of RTÉ's '1916 Road Show', a *History Ireland* Hedge School, chaired by editor **Tommy Graham**, convened in the Gresham Hotel, O'Connell Street, to discuss the proposition 'Was the Easter Rising Justified?', with **Felix Larkin** (academic director of the Parnell Summer School), **Ronan Fanning** (Professor Emeritus of Modern History, UCD), **Padraig Yeates** (trade union activist and author of *Lockout: Dublin 1913*) and **John Borgonovo** (UCC).

Below: The Easter Rising would not have met the five criteria set out by St Thomas Aquinas for a just war, according to Felix Larkin.

Not surprisingly, the answer was yes. And no.

Clearly, it's not a simple question. Justified how? On which criteria are we to make the assessment? Justified politically? Militarily? Morally? Could the 'Insurrection in Dublin' have had an initial legitimacy which it loses in retrospect? Conversely, can the end justify the means?

The panel discussion touched on many themes, such as the Rising's integral relationship to the First World War, partition, class, sovereignty and the nature of the state that emerged a few years later.

MORALITY

From this perspective, Felix Larkin was clear: no, the Easter Rising was not morally justified. He approached the issue with reference to Just War Theory, and in particular the thinking of Thomas Aquinas.

'Aquinas set out five criteria which would justify revolution, war, whatever. The first one is just cause. In the context of 1916, the government would have to have been a tyranny, without a legitimate title to rule Ireland. Second, violence must be a last resort: there is no other option for getting rid of the tyranny. Third, there should be a proportionality between the evil caused by a revolt and the evil that it aims to replace. Fourth, there should be a reasonable prospect of success; and fifth, the action should have the approval of the community at large. It is, frankly, doubtful whether even one of those criteria was met when the men of 1916 marched out on Easter Monday.

'And in the context of proportionality—on 9/11 there were 3,000 civilian casualties. That represented 0.037% of the population of New York in 2001. In 1916 the innocent civilian victims numbered 262, which represented a casualty rate of 0.08%, twice the casualty rate of 9/11. I think that puts Easter Week 1916 into perspective.'

This argument, however, was frankly dismissed by Prof. Ronan Fanning, the most recent biographer of de Valera.

'I don't think morality has got anything to do with it. I don't think Thomas Aquinas or any other Catholic theologian—or, come to that, a Buddhist thinker or thinker from any other religious group—has the right to sit in moral judgement on the events of the past. The responsibility of the historian, and it's a very difficult task, is to try to get as close as possible to saying what happened, why it happened and how it happened. It is not the responsibility of historians to arrogate to themselves the right to sit in moral judgement and to say this is good or this is bad. History is what it is.

'The significance of 1916 was that it was a seminal event which ultimately led to a larger measure of independence than we would otherwise have gained, certainly not as quickly and possibly not at all. That is why it is significant and, as far as I'm concerned, morality has got nothing whatever to do with it.'

But Larkin went back to the start. 'The question you asked us was, "Was 1916 justified?". As a historian, I agree that one's first responsibility is to understand what happened, but the question that was asked is whether it was justified. And we are faced in 2016 with a demand—or a request or an expectation—that we commemorate, and in some instances celebrate, 1916. Now commemoration and celebration imply to me approval, which implies a moral judgement or requires a moral judgement.

'If we have a celebration, if we have a commemoration, we are making a moral judgement. We are not acting as historians; we are acting as citizens.'

What of the 'tyranny' criterion required by Aquinas? Are there degrees of tyranny?

Larkin: 'Yes, there are gradations; history shows that. The tyranny of the Nazis is obviously much more serious, much more onerous, than anything the British Empire is alleged to have done.'

DEMOCRATIC MANDATE
But nobody voted for Patrick Pearse.

UCC's John Borgonovo introduced the question of political legitimacy.

'The Rising took place in the context of a world war which every combatant state, with the exception of Belgium, entered voluntarily, and where physical force was projected by every government involved. Another international context was empire, and if we're going to talk about morality—and I share Ronan's misgivings about that—then we should consider the morality of an empire that was holding one fifth of the world against its will. It may have been governed democratically within Britain, but not within India

or Africa or parts of Asia.

'We often look at the revolutionary period as a fight with Britain, but it was also a fight against empire. And from a pragmatic point of view, the Irish state came out with dominion status, something that wasn't on the cards in 1914. The Rising itself received overwhelming support, not only in the general election of 1918 but also in the 1920 local elections and the general election in 1921. So it seemed that the Irish people didn't have a problem with the Rising within a few years of the event itself.'

Larkin, however, had some reservations: 'In relation to 1918, I agree that the Sinn Féin platform in 1918 looked back to 1916, but it is not an unambiguous line. And to justify 1916 retrospectively by a retrospective electoral endorsement is a dangerous precedent, because it means that any crackpot minority of a minority—which is what these guys were in 1916—can come along and justify what they want to do by saying, "Ah, if you give us the chance to do this, in two years' time the electorate will see that we were right". Now, that undermines any democratic value that I hold dear.'

Fanning: 'Another point on the

democratic mandate issue is that general elections were suspended through the Great War. There was supposed to be a general election not later than 1915. That was suspended. Sinn Féin had begun to win by-elections, most famously East Clare in 1917. The 1918 general election was the first opportunity for the wisdom—or unwisdom—of John Redmond's line in respect of the First World War to be put to the electorate. It was the first opportunity for the people to speak.'

INTERNATIONAL CONTEXT
Padraig Yeates, journalist, trade unionist and author of a series of books on Dublin during the revolutionary period, set out a European context. How does an avowed socialist like James Connolly, who is seen as a great leader not only of the Rising but also of Irish Labour, fit in?

Yeates: 'Connolly was a great figure and intellectually he towered above the others. Yet how can we explain the alliance of this self-pro-

●

Above: John Redmond addressing the 'monster meeting' in support of the Home Rule bill on Sackville (O'Connell) Street on 31 March 1912. Eoin MacNeill and Patrick Pearse also spoke. (National Library of Ireland)

fessed socialist with physical-force nationalism? The international context provides a clue. If you look at countries like Austria-Hungary, they fragmented fairly quickly in the war; neither Germany nor Britain did. The Germans stuck it out until eventually starved into submission. There was a homogeneity in those countries.

'Ireland, on the other hand, was closer to the Austro-Hungarian model than to the western European one. In the former you find nationalists and socialists coalescing. It happened among the Poles and Czechs, for example. Both nationalists and socialists saw a once-in-a-lifetime opportunity to get rid of what they saw as an oppressive establishment. In Ireland, the Redmondite vision began to fade very quickly. Redmond took a gamble and it didn't pay off. Redmond represented the most myopic, the least ambitious, view of what we as a people were capable of.

'For example, in the early twentieth century there were concerted efforts to bring institutions run by religious orders under the cover of the Factory Acts, but they were resisted successfully by Redmond and the Irish Party. Imagine if factory inspectors had been able to go into Magdalen laundries before the First World War and say, "How much are you paid? What hours are you working?" Would those institutions have remained open?'

Borgonovo: 'During the war, the burden on ordinary people kept rising month after month—not just soldiers dying at the front, but hunger, shortages, inflation: life for ordinary people everywhere got worse. All combatants were under this stress. Those with the least democratic legitimacy experienced popular revolts. Unpopular regimes, like Tsarist Russia, collapsed; Finns mobilised and rebelled against Russia, Poles against Germany, Czechs against Austria-Hungary.

'And in the UK and the British Empire, it breaks out in Ireland. They also get a lot of trouble in India. There's trouble in Africa, in Nigeria, and Egypt starts rising up. All around the world, all these places where people are unhappy with their lot, they seize the opportunity to strike.'

VIOLENCE AS LAST RESORT?
What was the fundamental difference between the rhetoric of constitutional nationalism and revolutionary nationalism?

Fanning: 'This is where I think that the Tories understood what the Irish nationalist demand was and the Liberals didn't. The Irish demand was for separation of some sort. Now we call it independence; in O'Connell's time it was Repeal, for a Fenian in the 1860s it was a "republic", for Parnell (who says "No man has the right to set a boundary to the march of the nation") it was Home Rule. Or you can call it "the Republic".

'But at what point does the Republic become tangible? De Valera said that the first time he ever heard mention of "the Republic" was when he heard Patrick McCartan, a hard-line IRB man, make a public speech some time in 1912 extolling the virtues of a republic. Years later, following a chat with McCartan after dinner in New York or somewhere in America in 1919, de Valera recalled how he went home that night and thought to himself, "That's a very fine idea, a republic, but it's utterly unrealistic". And we know where he ended up!'

Larkin: 'And, interestingly, McCartan was opposed to the 1916 Rising because it wasn't even sanctioned or organised by the IRB as such but by the military council of the IRB, which was a subset of the IRB. So to say that the Rising was instigated by a minority of a minority of a minority is no exaggeration.

'And it is artificial to postulate that the conflict was between, on the one hand, Redmond, who I accept was in decline, and revolution on the streets of Dublin on the other. There were other political options. Just because Redmond has shot his bolt doesn't justify a revolution that involved the deaths of 485 people.'

FAILURE OF PARLIAMENTARY DEMOCRACY
The Irish people had been voting solidly for Home Rule, for 'separation', since the 1870s, but by one means or another this was stymied at Westminster.

Fanning: 'This is absolutely true, because what happens is that violence triumphs because British parliamentary democracy fails in Ireland. Asquith said this in a letter to the king in the autumn of 1913. He said, you know, if the Home Rule Act is not enacted next year, if it doesn't come to pass, I dread to think what is going to happen in Ireland, it will become absolutely ungovernable except by the methods which will offend the conscience of Britain and the conscience of the dominions. And that's exactly what happened when the Black and Tans started to run amok in 1920.'

Borgonovo: 'Physical force is deployed and is successful in the Home Rule crisis. The Ulster Volunteer Force is successful; it works. And then when we talk about the Easter Rising, it works, it worked.'

Larkin: 'But that is basically "the end justifies the means" and that's an appalling principle.'

Fanning: 'It's not a principle, Felix, it's a fact.' [Laughter.]

Larkin: 'Yes, all right, if you're arguing, Ronan, that the Rising was an evil necessity, I go a certain distance with you on that. But I'm not prepared …'

Fanning: 'I wouldn't say evil.'

Larkin: 'No, I was thinking … I don't want to get caught up in a Catholic kind of thinking, but I was thinking, in relation to the Easter theme, that there is a part of the Easter ceremony where they sing the *Exsultet*, and one of the lines is, "O happy fault, O necessary sin of Adam that earns so great a redeemer". Are we arguing the same thing, that the happy fault of 1916 gave us our independence, which may or may not be great?'

Yeates: 'To move it forward slightly—it was Michael Collins who said that the treaty didn't create an independent Ireland but it created the conditions in which it was possible to achieve freedom, and that's the fundamental difference between what was available, or what people thought was available, in 1914 as Irish nationalists and what actually was available in 1921–22.

'Also, any of you who have read lots of witness statements will see, time and again, that people aren't talking about economic issues or material issues generally; they're talking about saving the soul of a country. As Ronan said, we've evolved to a stage that people had enough confidence to vote themselves into the European Union; it's an absolutely vital point and one we tend to forget.'

EXECUTIONS

If the leaders hadn't been shot, would the Rising have succeeded?

Fanning: 'Well, shooting the leaders was a mistake; the British government realised that it was a mistake but they realised it too late. Because they had got out of the habit of executing the leaders of Irish revolutions: 1803, Robert Emmet, yes; but Young Irelanders, Fenians, 1860s, imprisonment, transportation, no executions.

'But that changed because of the circumstances of the Great War. The prime minister and his cabinet colleague had sons who'd been killed in the Great War, so the reference in the Rising Proclamation to "our gallant allies in Europe" was regarded as a stab in the back, as a great treachery. And they gave Maxwell powers to execute leaders in accordance with martial law.

'What's very interesting about Maxwell is that within weeks of his arrival here—and he is pursuing the policy of martial law and is carrying out the executions—he realises that rebellion is crystallising very quickly and very hard against the executions. So I think it's a very apposite question. If they had treated the leaders of the Rising the way they treated the leaders of the Fenian Rising of the 1860s the outcome might have been very different.'

Larkin: 'A further major factor in changing public opinion between 1916 and the general election in 1918 was, of course, the very real threat of conscription at the beginning of 1918. If you read through the newspapers of those years, public opinion was very evenly balanced until the conscription crisis in 1918. That absolutely wipes the Irish Parliamentary Party out and gives Sinn Féin the opportunity which it clearly took in the general election.'

SOVEREIGNTY

Borgonovo: 'One of the things about 1916, one of the goals seems to have been to get recognised as a belligerent, to fight basically on one side and to be recognised. There was already a recognition that there would be a post-war settlement and a peace conference, and there seems to have been an awareness among folks of the need, basically, to get in, and if Germany wins they're sorted and will be recognised post-war. There was an idea that things were up in the air and that everything was possible for this brief period of time.'

If Germany had won the war, would 'the rebels' have got a seat at the table?

Fanning: 'I don't think anybody can tell one way or another. It's just too unpredictable. I don't think that would have been a German priority, quite frankly.

'But it isn't 1916—1916 sows the seed, if you like. But the effect of violence, from the point of view of the impact it has on the British government, is the guerrilla war of 1921, and that leads to a situation where, by 1937, after de Valera comes back in the first place to power in 1932, Ireland is as independent as he, and the great majority of what were by that stage Irish Republicans, wanted it to be.

'Now, that degree of independence would never have been attained so quickly. It might never have been attained at all.

'Garret FitzGerald has written a couple of very interesting essays in a book called *Reflections on the Irish State* in which he says that this was the last moment at which Irish inde-

pendence could be effectively achieved and really be effective.

'Just one point which is key here: we would never have had the nerve to say that we know what it is to be sovereign. We *have* our sovereignty; we've been there, got the T-shirt, we're prepared to enter the European Community in 1972: 83% of voters voted in favour. They wouldn't have been prepared to do that, to agree to the surrender of sovereignty involved in that, if they hadn't been satisfied that Irish sovereignty was secured.'

●

Above: Garret FitzGerald believed that this was the last moment at which Irish independence could be effectively achieved and really be effective. (William Murphy)

> 'One of the things about 1916, one of the goals seems to have been to get recognised as a belligerent, to fight basically on one side and to be recognised.'

It is **'a humbling experience to see such an extraordinary appetite for history as has been shown today and is shown again and again in this country by people's interest in their past.'**

PARTITION

Larkin: 'There's no reference to partition in the 1916 Proclamation. It's just regarded as something that is not going to happen. But it had already … it was inevitable by then, it was absolutely inevitable. There was nothing Sinn Féin in the 1920–21 period could do about partition. If you take de Valera's document number two, he doesn't complain once about the Ulster clauses in the treaty, not once. The attitude to partition among many nationalists and Republicans has always been that it is an evil, it has to be denounced and it has to be ended. And what that is fundamentally based on is a refusal to allow Ulster unionists the same right to self-determination that Irish nationalists demanded for themselves.'

Borgonovo: 'But that was a grievance from the outset. It was accepted as a reality [only] because of the British intervention. But partition was seen as unfair and it was also seen as denying the economic future of the state, because Belfast was the industrial and financial centre of the island.

'So I actually think that the recognition that partition was the inevitable solution that was going to be enforced by Britain was one of the driving forces behind the rise of Sinn Féin. That arouses the sense of grievance that constitutionalism had failed so utterly.'

HISTORIAN V. CITIZEN

Fanning: 'I find it a humbling experience to see such an extraordinary appetite for history as has been shown today and is shown again and again in this country by people's interest in their past. I'm one of the editors—we've now done ten volumes—of a thing called 'The Documents on Irish Foreign Policy'. It's not cheap, but the US State Department, which does the comparable series, are utterly amazed that there are citizens who go into the bookshops and buy this for themselves. They wouldn't dream of trying to sell it to citizens. They just farm it out to libraries and that's it.

'So I think the queues today, the discussion today … I mean, to see people come in and queue in the hotel, to queue outside here, is a really humbling and rewarding experience, and I think all historians are very grateful for the kind of public interest there is. I found this a very interesting discussion today and I'd like to conclude by simply thanking you all very much indeed.'

The full discussion can be heard at: www.historyireland.com/hedge-schools/

Below: If Maxwell (centre) had treated the leaders of the Rising the way the leaders of the Fenian Rising of the 1860s had been treated the outcome might have been very different. (RTÉ Stills Library)

BOOKS

REWRITING THE RISING

BY **JOHN GIBNEY**

A brief round-up of historical writing and the state of scholarship on the Rising on its centenary

The Easter Rising has been revered, revised and reviled. It is widely assumed that the 50th anniversary of the Rising in 1966 was an unalloyed festival of adulation (the 75th anniversary was a different proposition, a notoriously muted affair that took place against the shadow of the modern Troubles). Much of what happened in 1966 was indeed adulatory, but to assume that *all* of it was ignores an awkward reality: the 50th anniversary also prompted a wave of scholarly research by figures such as the late F.X. Martin that opened the door to more critical and nuanced assessments of the Rising and which has stood the test of time (to find out how 1916 was marked in 1966, see Roisín Higgins's excellent *Transforming 1916*).

F.X. Martin's essays from the 1960s were founded on the most basic principle of historical scholarship: examining new or overlooked sources. The same applies today with the release in recent years of two crucially important collections: the Bureau of Military History (BMH) Witness Statements, released in 2003, and the continuing release since 2011 of the Military Service Pensions Collection (MSPC). The latter have yet to be fully integrated into writing on the Rising, but the BMH

testimonies have become a staple and have shaped two of the standard modern accounts. Charles Townshend's substantial *Easter 1916*, perhaps more than any other work, sets the Rising into its fullest context, while Fearghal McGarry's elegant and vivid *The Rising* uses the BMH statements to much fuller effect and, in doing so, essentially rewrites the story as 'history from below'. Both are reissued for the centenary. Mention should also be made of McGarry's companion volume, *Rebels*, which collates the BMH statements on 1916 in a user-friendly manner.

With regard to the 'big picture', two recent works come to mind. Roy Foster's beautifully written *Vivid faces* dissects the revolutionary generation in remarkable detail and fleshes out a new generation of nationalist activists, many of whom took part in 1916 and much more besides. It does concentrate, quite sympathetically, on the more respectable middle classes, and, oddly, the section on the Rising is not as strong (there might have been a smaller book waiting to get out). But Foster is far too good a historian not to read. That said, it does not offer a fundamental reinterpretation of 1916.

On the other hand, the first volume of Padraig Yeates's remarkable trilogy on revolutionary Dublin, *A city in wartime*, views the Rising as just one phenomenon among many: Yeates's concentration on the effect of the First World War on the Irish capital has implications for the manner in which the shift in public sympathy took place. Here, it was not

simply that the light dawned on Irish people who suddenly became republicans; instead, socio-economic conditions and an unpopular war helped to shift allegiance from Redmondite nationalism to separatism. This is flagged in Townshend's book: that the Irish Party lost fatal momentum after 1914 as Home Rule rested in the statute book, and lost support as the war took a dreadful toll.

From the context of the event, we can move to the event itself. More general accounts have been produced in recent times, often to a high standard. Shane Kenna's *Conspirators* is a heavily illustrated account of the Irish Republican Brotherhood, while an up-to-date, accessible and lavishly produced overview of the Rising itself is Conor McNamara's *The Easter Rebellion: a new illustrated history*, which draws upon substantial research. A more populist account is Turtle Bunbury's *Easter dawn*, another attractively produced and well-illustrated account. Michael Barry's handsome photo-history, *Courage boys, we are winning*, covers a wide range of material: Barry's own contemporary photographs of sites associated with the Rising are especially useful. Finally, Derek Molyneux and Darren Kelly's *When the clock struck in 1916* offers a vivid and accessible account from the perspective of the combatants. Historians may baulk at the authors' dramatic elements of creative non-fiction, but the authors point this out at the outset of an immensely readable and evocative account from a distinct perspective.

That every local authority in the

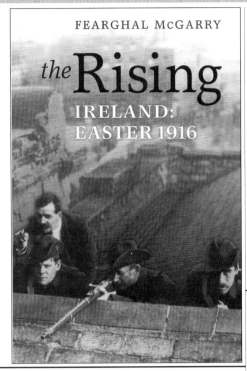

FEARGHAL McGARRY

the Rising

IRELAND: EASTER 1916

the garrisons. A similar but far more detailed account of the most famous garrison of all is contained in Jimmy Wren's *The GPO garrison, Easter Week 1916: a biographical dictionary*. This remarkable work, the product of decades of research, provides a biography (many of which are illustrated by the author) of each of the 572 men and women whom the author estimates were in the GPO (it would hardly fill Croke Park). He also tries to quantify his subjects: strikingly, 41% of those who fought in the GPO were neutral in the Civil War six years later. Works such as these

are essential for those who would seek to reach their own understanding of the Rising.

The same could be said of two anthologies: Mairéad Ashe Fitzgerald's *A terrible beauty: poetry of 1916* (which is unfortunately let down by a poor introduction), and *Handbook of the Irish Revival*, edited by Declan Kiberd and P.J. Mathews. This chunky tome allows the Rising generation—from cultural activists to some who fought—to speak in their own words, and is an essential read to understand the cultural, intellectual and political backdrop.

country has devised a 2016 programme might give the impression that the Rising took place across the country. It most certainly did not. Two local groups in Dublin's north inner city have produced impressive publications on their areas: *Our Rising: Cabra and Phibsborough in Easter 1916*, by Brian Hanley and Donal Fallon, and *The 1916 Rising in Stoneybatter, Smithfield and the Markets*, by the Stoneybatter and Smithfield People's History Project.

The material culture of the time is the subject of scholarly scrutiny in *Making 1916*, edited by Lisa Godson and Joanna Brück, which covers a remarkable range of topics, from the clothing of the insurgents to the National Museum's old 1916 exhibition. Lorcan Collins's *1916: the Rising handbook* is a modern equivalent to the famous *Sinn Féin Rebellion Handbook* published by the *Irish Times*, complete with time-lines, documents, lists of participants and prisoners, details of weapons and locations, and much else besides.

Joe Connell's two works, *Dublin Rising 1916* and *Who's who in the Easter Rising*, provide, respectively, a detailed gazetteer of virtually every Dublin location and a biographical account of everyone who fought in

COURAGE BOYS, WE ARE WINNING
An Illustrated History of the 1916 Rising

MICHAEL BARRY

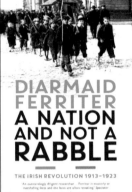

DIARMAID FERRITER
A NATION AND NOT A RABBLE
THE IRISH REVOLUTION 1913–1923

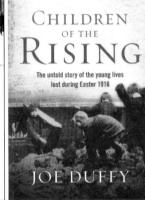

CHILDREN OF THE RISING
The untold story of the young lives lost during Easter 1916

JOE DUFFY

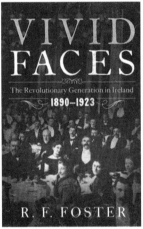

VIVID FACES
The Revolutionary Generation in Ireland 1890–1923

R. F. FOSTER

A Woven Silence
MEMORY, HISTORY & REMEMBRANCE

FELICITY HAYES-McCOY

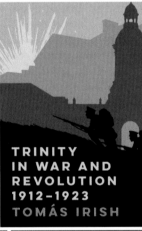

TRINITY IN WAR AND REVOLUTION 1912–1923
TOMÁS IRISH

CONSPIRATORS
A Photographic History of Ireland's Revolutionary Underground

Shane Kenna

HANDBOOK OF THE IRISH REVIVAL
Edited by Declan Kiberd and P.J. Mathews
An anthology of Irish Cultural and Political Writings 1891–1922

16LIVES
MICHAEL O'HANRAHAN

Conor Kostick

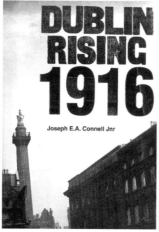

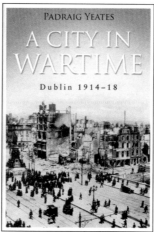

WORKS CITED

Mairéad Ashe Fitzgerald, *A terrible beauty: poetry of 1916* (O'Brien Press, €14.99 hb, ISBN 97818471735).

Michael Barry, *Courage boys, we are winning* (Andalus Press, €25 hb, ISBN 9780956038395).

Turtle Bunbury, *Easter dawn: the 1916 Rising* (Mercier, €29.99 hb, ISBN 9781781172582).

Lorcan Collins, *1916: the Rising handbook* (O'Brien Press, €14.99 pb, ISBN 9781847175991).

Joseph E.A. Connell, *Dublin Rising 1916* (Wordwell, €19 hb, ISBN 9781905569908).

Joseph E.A. Connell, *Who's who in the Dublin Rising 1916* (Wordwell, €19 hb, ISBN 9781905569946).

Joe Duffy, *Children of the Rising: the untold story of the young lives lost during Easter 1916* (Hachette Ireland, €19.99 hb, ISBN 9781473617056).

R.F. Foster, *Vivid faces: the revolutionary generation in Ireland, 1890–1923* (Penguin, £20 pb, ISBN 9780241954249).

Lisa Godson and Joanna Brück (eds), *Making 1916: material and visual culture of the Easter Rising* (Liverpool University Press, £25 hb, ISBN 9781781381229).

Brian Hanley and Donal Fallon, *Our Rising: Cabra and Phibsborough in Easter 1916* (Cabra 1916 Rising Committee).

Felicity Hayes-McCoy, *A woven silence: memory, history and remembrance* (Collins Press, €14.99 pb, ISBN 9781848892521).

Roisín Higgins, *Transforming 1916: meaning, memory and the fiftieth anniversary of the Easter Rising* (Cork University Press, €25 pb, ISBN 9781782050575).

Tomás Irish, *Trinity in war and revolution, 1912–1923* (Royal Irish Academy, €30 hb, ISBN 9781908996787).

Shane Kenna, *Conspirators: a photographic history of Ireland's revolutionary underground* (Mercier Press, €14.99 pb, ISBN 9781781173541).

Declan Kiberd and P.J. Mathews, *Handbook of the Irish Revival: an anthology of Irish cultural and political writings, 1891–1923* (Abbey

The O'Brien Press has produced its '16 Lives' series of biographies. The Royal Irish Academy has also trawled through its enormous *Dictionary of Irish biography* and extracted 42 biographies, from the signatories to Home Rulers, British officials and some of its chroniclers (Joe Lee's piece on Patrick Pearse is essential reading). These have now been illustrated with distinctive black-and-white 'scraperboard' images by David Rooney and published as *1916: portraits and lives*, edited by James Quinn and Laurence White. This beautiful production is topped and tailed with a wide-ranging and provocative introduction and afterword by Patrick Maume, and is at once a work of reference and an essential overview of 1916.

Another beautifully produced and superbly written work of group biography is Fearghal McGarry's *The Abbey rebels*, which explores the lives of seven individuals associated with the Abbey Theatre (such as Peader Kearney and Helena Molony). Unlike many of the works under discussion here, it looks forward to examine their lives after. In doing so it explores more than just 1916.

For those who like to read *as Gaeilge*, Coisceim have produced a number of Irish-language titles. One well worth reading is *Mícheál Ó Mealláin* by his son Séamus Ó Mealláin.

Familial perspectives are provided in Sinéad McCoole's *Easter widows*, a group study of the families of the executed leaders (and also a notable contribution to the study of Irishwomen's experience in the revolution). Felicity Hayes-McCoy explores the legacy of the revolution in relation to her family in *A woven silence*, while Helene O'Keeffe's *To speak of Easter Week* has its origins in oral history and examines the lore passed down veterans' families.

The human cost of the violence is at the heart of Joe Duffy's enormously readable *Children of the Rising*. This humane book does not discriminate between those children killed by one side or the other but acts as a social history of Dublin (though the poor quality of its illustrations is a major let-down).

Another overlooked group consists of those Irishmen who fought in the British army: Neil Richardson explores their experiences of the fighting in Dublin in *According to their lights*.

Finally, how the Rising was intertwined with two very different institutions is explored in publications that range far beyond 1916: the superb *The GAA and revolution in Ireland*, edited by Gearóid Ó Tuathaigh, and Tomás Irish's lavish *Trinity in war and revolution*. The latter work is especially notable, as TCD could be said to represent a very different Ireland outside the nationalist tradition; indeed, it became a British barracks during Easter Week. This well-written and well-researched study sheds valuable light on the experience of traditions in Irish life that had little or no sympathy for the rebels or for the revolution that ultimately came in its wake.

IRELAND'S CULTURE IN THREE TITLES

To subscribe to any of these titles (and to avail of a discount) contact us directly at:

SUBSCRIPTIONS DEPT:

WORDWELL LTD
Unit 9, 78 Furze Road,
Sandyford Industrial Estate,
Dublin 18, Ireland

PHONE:

+353-1-2933568
or email: office@wordwellbooks.com
or buy online at:
www.wordwellbooks.com

Theatre, €18.99 hb, ISBN 9780993180002).

Sinéad McCoole, *Easter widows: seven Irish women who lived in the shadow of the Easter Rising* (Doubleday Ireland, £14.99 pb, ISBN 9781781620236).

Fearghal McGarry, *The Rising: Ireland, Easter 1916 (centenary edition)* (Oxford University Press, £20 hb, ISBN 9780198732341).

Fearghal McGarry, *Rebels: voices from the Easter Rising* (Penguin, €14.69 pb, ISBN 9780141041278).

Fearghal McGarry, *The Abbey rebels of 1916: a lost revolution* (Gill, €29.99 hb, ISBN 9780717168811).

Conor McNamara, *The Easter Rebellion: a new illustrated history* (Collins Press, €24.99 hb, ISBN 9781848892590).

Derek Molyneux and Darren Kelly, *When the clock struck in 1916: close-quarter combat in the Easter Rising* (Collins Press, €17.99 pb, ISBN 9781848892132).

Helene O'Keeffe, *To speak of Easter Week: family memories of the Irish revolution* (Mercier Press, €25 hb, ISBN 9781781172216).

Séamus Ó Mealláin, *Mícheál Ó Mealláin* (Coisceim, €7.50 pb).

Gearóid Ó Tuathaigh (ed.), *The GAA and revolution in Ireland, 1913–1923* (Collins Press, €29.99 hb, ISBN 9781848892345).

James Quinn and Laurence White (eds), *1916: portraits and lives* (Royal Irish Academy, €30 hb, ISBN 9781908996381).

Neil Richardson, *According to their lights: stories of Irishmen in the British Army, Easter 1916* (Collins, €19.99 pb, ISBN 9781848892149).

Stoneybatter and Smithfield People's History Project, *The 1916 Rising in Stoneybatter, Smithfield and the Markets* (no details).

Charles Townshend, *Easter 1916: the Irish Rebellion* (2nd edn, Penguin, £10.68 pb, ISBN 9780141982472).

Jimmy Wren, *The GPO garrison, Easter Week 1916* (Geography Publications, €29.95 hb, ISBN 9780906602744).

Padraig Yeates, *A city in wartime: Dublin 1914–18* (Gill, €16.99 pb, ISBN 9780717154616).

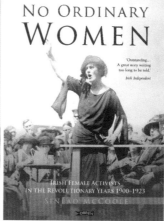
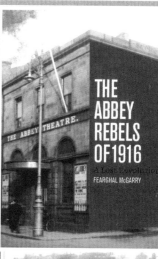
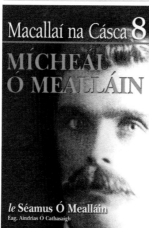
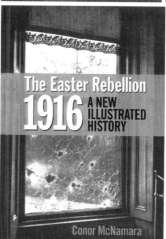
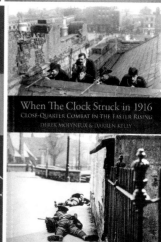
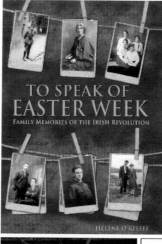

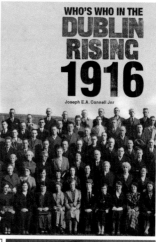

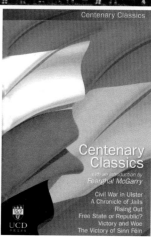

POSTSCRIPT

We will leave the last word to Éamonn Ceannt, writing on the eve of his execution

'IRELAND WILL HONOUR THOSE WHO RISKED ALL FOR HER HONOUR AT EASTER IN 1916'

On 7 May, the day before he was executed, Éamonn Ceannt wrote a letter to the Irish people that seems to sum up the bravery, determination, humanity and idealism of those who took part in the Rising. Some slight irony can be read into his comments, with the benefit of hindsight, as regards the future for Ireland and our current diffidence on the question of commemorating these events.

'I leave for the guidance of other revolutionaries, who may tread the path which I have trod, this advice, never to treat with the enemy, never to surrender to his mercy, but to fight to a finish. I see nothing gained, but grave disaster caused, by the surrender which has marked the end of the Irish Insurrection of 1916—so far at least as Dublin is concerned. The enemy has not cherished one generous thought for those who, with little hope, with poor equipment, and weak in numbers, withstood his forces for one glorious week. Ireland has shown she is a Nation. This generation can claim to have raised sons as brave as any that went before. And in the years to come, Ireland will honour those who risked all for her honour at Easter in 1916. I bear no ill will against whom I have fought. I have found the common soldiers and the higher officers human and companionable, even the English who were actually in the fight against us. Thank God soldiering for Ireland has opened my heart and made me see poor humanity where I expected to see only scorn and reproach. I have met the man who escaped from me by a ruse under the Red Cross. But I do not regret having withheld my fire. He gave me cakes!

I wish to record the magnificent gallantry and fearless, calm determination of the men who fought with me. All, all were simply splendid. Even I knew no fear nor panic and shrank from no risk, as I shrink not now from the death which faces me at daybreak. I hope to see God's face even for a moment in the morning. His will be done. All here are very kind. My poor wife saw me yesterday and bore up—so my warden told me—even after she left my presence. Poor Áine, poor Ronan. God is their only shield now that I am removed. And God is a better shield than I. I have just seen Áine, Nell, Richard and Mick and bade them a conditional good-bye. Even now they have hope.'

Left: Éamonn Ceannt, executed on 8 May 1916: 'I wish to record the magnificent gallantry and fearless, calm determination of the men who fought with me. All, all were simply splendid.' (National Library of Ireland)